# Four Traditions, One Spirit

# Four Traditions
# One Spirit

Chet Meyers

**North Star Press of St. Cloud, Inc.**
St. Cloud, Minnesota

Permissions:

The author gratefully acknowledges the generosity of Mary Oliver for permission to reprint two poems, "Praying" and "Wild Geese."

In addition he thanks Daniel Ladinsky for granting the use of certain lines of poetry and references to his books of poetry by Hafiz.

Finally, a special thanks to Coleman Barks for his permission and open-ended generosity to allow use of his wonderful translations of Rumi and Hafiz.

The author has chosen to donate all royalties from the sale of this book to The Lift Garage, a non-profit auto repair shop in Minneapolis that provides low-cost car repair to low-income Minnesotans.

Published by :
North Star Press of St. Cloud, Inc.
P.O. Box 451
St. Cloud, Minnesota 56302

northstarpress.com

# Table of Contents

# Acknowledgments

No one crafts a book without a lot of help from others. Two of my most invaluable resources have been students and fellow colleagues at Metropolitan State University, who taught me so very much the past four decades. I also thank the women and men whom I have been honored to know through many years of work in 12-Step programs. Then there were the Quaker elders of the Minneapolis Friends Meeting, who parented both my wife and me during the rather tumultuous 1970s; therapists, counselors, and spiritual directors who alternately held my hand and kicked my butt; and the ongoing fellowship of the Spirit of St. Stephens's Catholic Community, whose courage and resourcefulness are astounding. Blessings to those who read earlier drafts of chapters; you straightened me out when I would have lost the reader, or when too much ego interposed itself. And special thanks to Leah, Sue, and Michelle, who made my hope a reality.

Thanks to those who have crossed over to that other shore and who schooled me in their graceful writings: Thomas Merton, for teaching me that faith and reason need not be at war with each other; Albert Camus, for sustaining me during graduate school with his honesty, passion, and love of nature; the great Sufi poets Jellaludin Rumi and Hafiz, for stretching my rather limited concept of the Divine; Bill Coffin, my chaplain at seminary, for "afflicting my comfort" during the Vietnam War; and Jim Egan, who walked the spiritual road with me during my nervous breakthrough and introduced me to the richness of Lakota spirituality.

And thanks to the living: Robert Bly, whose poetry and writings taught me much about what it means to be a man; my dear, dear friends Catherine Warrick and Carol Holmberg, who continue to hold me up on this life-long spiritual journey and are 'tough' editors; brother Pat Carnes who wisely introduced me to 12-Step groups back in 1983; and two exceptional men, Ed Flahavan and Patrick Griffin, who showed me, by living it, the best of their faith tradition.

Blessings to my loving mom, dad, sister, and our extended family, who did a pretty good of job letting me set my own course in life, and to Mother Nature and a multitude of wild critters who have accepted me as kin, offering both joy and consolation on a daily basis.

Finally, I thank my dear wife, Miriam, my best friend, lover, and critic (not easy edges to walk), who has edited my writing the past thirty years and is usually right. Blessings on her for sticking with me through the nervous breakthrough years and the subsequent reconstruction of our marriage and for sharing with me a great love of silence, music, justice, the good earth, and critters large and small.

# Preface

Before you purchase a book, you should have at least a rough idea what it is about and, equally important, what it is not about. This is a book about hope—hope for the human condition. It is a hope for community and common cause that I believe is reflected in the spiritual traditions undergirding much of our present cultural diversity. In an age when human discourse and politics seem characterized by so much strife, divisiveness, and downright mean-spiritedness, it's difficult to find an environment of civility that reflects compassion and concern for the common good. Sadly, some of the most hostile expressions of discontent are often driven by religious insensibilities. And, yet, ironically, the great spiritual traditions all have much more in common than they do in conflict. When one sets aside religious arguments, statements of dogma, and fundamentalist interpretations, an amazing consensus of values and unity of purpose emerges from the spiritual traditions of Judaism, Christianity, Islam, and much of the wisdom of Native American people. These different traditions demonstrate a common human longing for love, compassion, and justice rooted in a mysterious, yet benevolent, transcendent force—God, Yahweh, Allah, or Great Mystery.

This book is not written to convince anyone of the existence of such a god or transcendent power. Rather, it is for those of us who already believe—no matter how faintly—in the existence of some transcendent power for good, but who also struggle with depressing daily events and a loss of the sense of that common good in a culture where conflict and animosity too often take center stage. Indeed, one of the primary struggles in any spiritual life is reconciling one's belief in the goodness of Ultimate Reality with the conflicts, tragedies, and vagaries of everyday life. If God is good, why do chaos and evil seem so present in the human community? There is no easy resolution to this tension. Don't expect any in what follows. Instead, please join me and men and women from a variety of spiritual traditions in a journey of faith and doubt, of hope and despair, that demonstrates an astounding unity of spiritual wisdom and longing for community.

# Chapter 1
# God-Language and Metaphor

*God as the ultimate mystery of being is beyond thinking.*

Joseph Campbell

Where to begin? From the outset difficult problems surround any discussion of a god, spirit, or transcendent force. One of the most serious dilemmas is that the very word "god" brings up thoughts, images, and deep-seated feelings from childhood. These images and feelings stay with us well into adulthood. Many Americans, regardless of background, grew up with a rather uniform image of God. In my own Protestant rearing, the image presented was of an almighty white male, in a long white robe, and seated high in heaven on a throne. This God loved me, but also had a quiver of lightning bolts nearby that He could toss my way if I got out of line—a sort of celestial Santa Claus, rewarding the good and punishing the bad, but more than that, directing everything that happens. That ambivalent image—of a loving, yet punishing, all-powerful God—stayed with me well beyond childhood, as, I would argue, it does for many religious believers.

It may help to pause a moment and try to recapture a few images of God you grew up with as a child. What feelings do you associate with your earliest images of the Divine? Sometimes, if we are fortunate, these feelings are comforting and nurturing. Often, however, old images of the Transcendent are less helpful and instill only fear and uncertainty in us. If you grew up in an environment free from religious beliefs, it's still a good bet you have some concept of a god in your mind. Indeed, most atheists I know have a powerfully negative image of the god they do *not* believe in.

A few years ago I attended a lecture by former Catholic priest John Dominic Crossan. He posed a simple question that left most in the audience in stunned silence. First he asked us to reconstruct an image of

1

God from our childhood. He paused, then asked, "How would you like to meet that God in a dark alley?"[1] Silence! How would you feel about meeting your childhood God in a dark alley? If your God was primarily the source of judgment and punishment, or if you were taught that God was responsible for everything that happens, including natural catastrophes, you probably wouldn't turn into that dark alley. Yet images of God, as the all-powerful cause or source of everything we experience, are still alive and well, and their roots go deep into western religion and culture. Indeed, the image of God as the Primary Cause still predominates in the Judeo/Christian/Islamic traditions. And, if we image the Transcendent as omnipotent and all-powerful, it makes sense to credit that Transcendent as the source of all that happens—the good the bad, and the ugly. What we forget is that *this is but one image* of the Transcendent. And perhaps not the most helpful. Even back in the fourteenth century, the Christian mystic Meister Eckhart was wary of the god of punishment and disasters. He complained, "How long will grown men and women . . . keep drawing in their coloring books an image of God that makes them sad?"[2]

One of our tasks then is to expand our present images, symbols, and metaphors of the Transcendent so that we might be enriched by the wisdom of others. So, as we begin to be open to alternative ways of thinking and feeling about the Transcendent, let's be willing to consider new words and images. As Woody Allen once wisely opined, "God is just dog spelled backwards."[3] I take his comment seriously. God is merely a word, "a word for a concept and power that is difficult, if not impossible, to put into words."[4] In what follows we will consider alternative words and images from a number of traditions—the Transcendent, Great Mystery, Universal Love, the Friend, the Divine, Higher Power, Ultimate Reality, even George Lucas's *Star Wars* image of the Force. Why? Because old images and feelings often stand in the way of exploring alternative ways of thinking and feeling. The good news is that even midst the diversity of images and names from different traditions, we will discover a consensus regarding the nature of a benevolent transcendent force at work in the universe. For I believe these spiritual traditions have all come to know the same Ultimate Reality, but through different names, images, and metaphors. Different names for god, different cultures, different stories, different practices, yet at their core an amazing agreement on human hopes and aspirations and the nature of the spiritual life.

A second problem in regard to God-language is that, if there is such a transcendent force at work in the universe, *it by definition transcends or goes beyond any rational, objective, scientific description.* That is, the Transcendent exceeds the ability of our minds to fully comprehend. As anthropologist Joseph Campbell wisely observed, "God as the ultimate mystery of being is beyond thinking."[5] This does not mean we need throw up our hands in despair. Nor do we have to sacrifice our brains and rigidly adhere to a dogma or set of beliefs in God as a cosmic manipulator. There is much we can learn from our personal experience and especially the wisdom traditions of others. After all, the choice of images we use is ours to make. Though we may never fully comprehend the Transcendent, and logic and science can never provide a definitive answer, we can expand our vision. And letting go of some of our old preconceptions, and admitting there are limits to what we know, can help open the door to new ways of seeing, thinking and feeling.

## Metaphors and drawing new pictures of God

So what to do? We can begin by accepting our rational limits and opening ourselves to new and expanded images of what Alcoholics Anonymous members call a Higher Power. Although, when traveling the spiritual road, we are limited to images and metaphors, some images help more than others. Some point to hope, and others to despair. As we explore different traditions, we discover spiritual women and men often find poetry, art, even song and dance, valuable tools when thinking, feeling, and talking about matters of the Spirit. The arts have always provided a powerful access to feelings and understandings that go beyond our poor prosaic attempts at definition.

Webster defines metaphor as using "a word or phrase . . . denoting one kind of object or idea . . . in place of another, to suggest a likeness or analogy between them," that is, a comparison between two words or objects in which one word or image is used to clarify another word or image.[6] English teachers consider metaphors figurative language, which suggests a comparison that helps us understand something at a deeper, often more expansive, level.

"The Lord is my shepherd, I shall not want . . ."[7]

23rd Psalm Hebrew scriptures

"When I first started loving God I felt I had fallen into the ocean, but I was only standing on the shore . . ."[8]

Sufi poetry of Hafiz

Of course images age with time. We don't have much contact with shepherds any more, but two thousand years ago they were common and central figures in rural Israel. Their job was to protect the sheep, to lead them safely to better grazing land, and to guard them at night. The psalmist is not saying God *is* a shepherd, but that He/She is *like* a shepherd in the ways we are cared for. In the psalmist's day, feelings of being shepherded were easily associated with those of safety and consolation.

Similarly, when the Sufi poet Hafiz tries to convey what his first encounter with the Transcendent felt like, he is not saying God *is* the ocean, but God is *likened* to the ocean in its immensity. Then Hafiz deepens this metaphor by saying that in his first encounter with God he wasn't even close to experiencing the immense nature of this Transcendent Ocean. He was only getting his feet wet.

Metaphors like *shepherd* and *ocean* help us make sense out of things we may never fully understand at a rational or logical level. If we can let go of some of our preconceived ideas of who/what God is, we will still need to struggle with the nature of paradoxical (seemingly contradictory) language and images. But metaphors and figurative language can help us better grasp some of the paradoxes that arise in any discussion of the Transcendent. And lest we think metaphors are not as forceful as reason and logic, consider how frequently the "hard" sciences like astronomy, astrophysics and cosmology rely on metaphors and images to help communicate concepts like black holes, the Big Bang theory of creation, dwarf stars, and red giants.

As we explore this benevolent Force that exists midst a world of pain and tragedy, there will be surprises for all of us. The Sufi poet Rumi ends one of the poems about our limits to understanding the Transcendent with these lines "When you eventually see through the veils to how things really are, you will keep saying again and again, 'This is certainly not like we thought it was!'"[9] Likewise, the Lakota leader Black Elk reminds us of the limitations of our own cultural assumptions. In an interview with Joseph Epes Brown, Black Elk tells of his meetings with Christian white men and them telling him about Jesus and his redemptive act of dying on a cross and how he would arise from the dead. Black Elk does not contest their belief and says that he understands and knows it to be true ". . . but the white men should know that for the red people too it was the will of the Great Spirit that an animal turn itself into a two-legged person in order to bring the most holy pipe to His people."[10] He then tells the story of how the Lakota received the first "peace pipe" from White Buffalo Woman who, after giving the pipe, turns into a white buffalo. Which story is stranger—Christian or Lakota?

As we begin to consider alternative cultural images of God, we can also draw on our own personal experiences of the Transcendent and the experiences of seekers who went before us. It is important and edifying to read the literature of spirituality, but unless some of the truth others have perceived connects and makes sense with our own personal experiences, nothing much will change. You can read all the books you want about how to play golf, but until you pick up a club and begin hitting balls you are not really in the game. I know of few, if any, individuals who have been convinced by rational argument that Ultimate Reality is benevolent until they recognize that they have personally experienced the goodness of that Reality. And we will get no confirmation or consolation from empirical science on the existence of a benevolent God. It is not a *fact* we come to know, so much as something we experience. In the words of theologian Reinhold Niebuhr,

> The ultimate affirmation . . . about the goodness of God remains, of course, a hypothesis of faith which can never be proved to those who are preoccupied with the chaos and evil which life reveals; neither can it be disproved to those who have felt it validated in their inner experience.[11]

Niebuhr suggests that, despite the persistence of chaos and evil, the inner experience of healing, consolation, and love, following a tragedy, offers our most compelling evidence in support of a benevolent Higher Power. And, while we need to trust more in our own personal experiences, we still need to proceed with caution. In an era where "sharing" our lives through various social media is such a cultural expectation, it is wise to remember that we are not expected to be emotional exhibitionists. Some aspects of our lives still deserve respect and privacy. Personal experiences of the Transcendent are not meant to be shared widely and publicly, but we can find help in discerning those experiences by talking with a spiritual director or close friend journeying with us on the spiritual road.

Recognizing and trying to expand one's understanding of the Transcendent is not for the faint of heart. Nor is it for the muddle-headed. It is a struggle that requires patience, openness to complexity, and a realization that in the end we may have only proximate answers to our questions. Sadly, popular American culture, and especially the media, do little to support or to reinforce those attitudes of inquiry or any serious consideration of spiritual matters.

## Modern culture, the media, and spirituality

We live in a culture where the popular media exerts inordinate power and influence. I'll spare you a long sermon on the mindlessness of commercial television. Let's just say its themes, images, and dialogues do little to encourage patient, open, or in-depth thinking, let alone give any hint of true-to-life spiritual concerns. Commercial television incorporates speed, stereotypic gut-reaction images, and simplistic resolutions to problems. The same is true of local network news. Keep tabs sometime on the content of your evening local news. It's mostly bad news—natural disasters, car crashes, fires, abduction or rape, murder, and robbery—all delivered in rapid-fire sound bites with no attempt at in-depth coverage. And ironically, most of those news stories do not warrant any coverage at all.

Let's not forget the primary purpose of commercial television is the commercials. Of the twenty-four hours of television an average American viewer watches each week, eighteen minutes of every hour are dedicated to commercials. That works out to about forty-two commercials per hour and over seven hours of commercials each week. And those commercials are designed to convince us of the value of fast cars, perfectly proportioned bodies, unhealthy food that will soothe us, and an abundance of medications that will make us feel better. No time remains for struggle with complex issues if we spend our time looking for a quick fix.

Sorry, that almost was a sermon. The point of that little diatribe is that the popular media reinforces sloppy thinking and discourages any consideration of complex issues. As a result, simplistic and dualistic thinking dominates our political debates, and our public policy reflects such either/or thinking: we live in red or blue states, we are liberals or conservatives, hawks or doves. And the same thinking carries over to discussions of religion with noticeable overlap: we are either pro-life or pro-choice, straight or gay, we either believe in God or evolution. It is no wonder so many people hold on to simplistic images of the Transcendent. As a result, many people either do not believe in a god, because they cannot reconcile a loving god with daily tragedies, or, perhaps more sadly, they do believe in a god, and blame that god as the cause of all tragedies and bad news.

Those of us who affirm, and have at some time experienced, a benevolent Spirit or Higher Power must struggle with the persistence of tragedies and the bad things that happen in our own lives. This is a complex problem, one that will not be solved in this little treatise. It is, however, a problem that deserves our time and effort to grapple with. Just don't expect popular culture and the media to aid us in that struggle.

As we pursue our spiritual journey, the first task is to admit our human limitations in understanding the Divine. As theologian Sallie McFague has observed, any metaphor, image, or model we create to explain the Transcendent will, at some point, "miss the mark."[12] So we admit, from the outset, that the Transcendent is transcendent and we may never fully comprehend it. Next, it will be helpful to consider the richness of images and metaphors other cultures and disciplines offer regarding the nature of Ultimate Reality. If we can let go, or at least hold in abeyance, the images of God we had as children and entertain alternatives, we can broaden our spiritual vision. The task is not easy. But we can expand our present thoughts and feelings so our belief in goodness can exist midst the tragedies of everyday life. To do this we need to give ourselves permission to ask questions, to express doubts, and to be open to new ways of thinking and feeling with regard to a Higher Power—and maybe to cut back our media viewing. In the next chapter we will explore the surprising and uplifting themes and values common to our great Western spiritual traditions.

ᦙᕀᦙ

PLEASE READ: Each chapter ends with a brief writing exercise. Not much space is provided because most folks don't like writing in their books. The exercises are designed to be written because writing accesses another part of your brain. If you are compulsive, like I am, you may be tempted to skip these exercises. If so, try to set aside your reservations and work them . . . don't simply think them in your head.

This is not a long book and could easily be read rather quickly. Please take your time. As Grandma used to advise at meal time "Take it in small bites." And, because spirituality involves our emotions on a profound level, it might be helpful to share your work with a trusted friend, counselor or sponsor.

**Exercise #1 Your earliest image of God**

In the space below, try to draw a sketch of your earliest idea of God. Drawing an image can be helpful, for in doing so we use a different part of our brain than we do when writing. If you get stuck drawing something, simply write down a description. After doing that, look at what you have drawn or written and write a brief paragraph saying how it felt to grow up with that concept as a child.

Chapter 2

# The Nature of Ultimate Reality

*When you eventually see through the veils, to how things*
*really are you will keep saying again and again*
*"This is certainly not like we thought it was."*

Jelaluddin Rumi

I n 1984 a group of spiritual teachers representing very different religious
traditions met in Snowmass, Colorado, to explore common spiritual
concerns and themes. The group included Jewish, Buddhist, Tibetan
Buddhist, Hindu, Islamic, Native American, Russian Orthodox, Roman
Catholic, and Protestant spiritual leaders. It was convened by Father
Thomas Keating, a Catholic priest well known and respected for his work
on centering prayer. As the group shared their different spiritual traditions,
they discovered a surprising sense of unity and a number of principles on
which they could all agree. Consider the following points of agreement affirmed by these nine very different spiritual traditions.

> The world religions bear witness to the experience of Ultimate Re-
> ality, to which they give different names: Brahman, Allah, Absolute,
> God, Great Spirit.

> Ultimate Reality cannot be limited by any name or concept. Ulti-
> mate Reality may be experienced not only through religious prac-
> tices but also through nature, art, human relationships, and service
> to others.

> As long as the human condition is experienced as separate from
> Ultimate Reality, it is subject to ignorance and illusion, weakness,
> and suffering.[13]

That all these great spiritual traditions could come to such a consensus, I believe, is a powerful testimony to the unity of the world of

spirit. Ironically, about the same time as the Snowmass gathering (about which I knew nothing), I was granted a year's sabbatical by my university to develop a new course entitled Themes in Spirituality. To have a year free from teaching and advising, to read and prepare for a new course, was a luxury. I spent much of my time studying Judaism, Christianity, and Lakota Native American traditions. I also explored Zen Buddhism, Sufism, and contemporary feminist perspectives.

What most amazed me during this year of reading and reflection was how the same spiritual themes kept reappearing, time and time again. While the specific cultures, languages, images, and stories differed widely, at their core these great traditions all seemed in agreement on fundamental spiritual matters. These common themes, and the consensus of agreement at the Snowmass conference, confirmed for me an amazing unity of spiritual wisdom. And that, in turn, challenged me to consider alternative ways of thinking and feeling about my rather limited childhood images of God. Yet, at the same time I felt challenged, this unity seemed profoundly nurturing and familiar. It began to undergird my own spiritual life and greatly enrich my work with adult students.

But before moving on to consider what others have thought, said, and prayed regarding Ultimate Reality, it's important to ground ourselves in our own personal experience. It is a challenge to reconsider old ways of thinking about anything, let alone the nature of God. We can explore what others have said, but if we have no personal experience to which we can relate these spiritual themes, our attempts to consider new images and metaphors of the Transcendent will bear little fruit.

### Experiencing the transcendent

In all my teaching and discussions of faith with adult students, I can't recall anyone who was ever convinced of the existence of a transcendent realm by words, logic, or reason. One comes to believe in transcendence only when one has experienced it and recognized that one has experienced it. Grappling with the Transcendent is not merely a head trip—something we come to know on a cognitive level. It is only through both our heads, and more importantly our hearts, that we can ever make sense of *the paradox of a benevolent transcendent force that exists alongside the reality of human tragedy and suffering.* And, in that process of putting head and heart together, we may need help discerning the nature of transcendent experiences.

Sometimes our preconceptions of what we think is transcendent are so grand that we do not appreciate everyday encounters with Ultimate Reality. At the beginning of the course Themes in Spirituality I asked my students to complete a brief writing exercise to help initiate our discussion of transcendence. The assignment read:

> Please take a few minutes to write down one time during the past year that you were powerfully aware of a transcendent force that seemed larger than the material world and that lifted you, as it were, out of your normal everyday fears and concerns; a time when you felt peaceful or at rest in the presence of something much larger than you.

My university teaching was primarily done in the state of Minnesota. In northern Minnesota is an incredibly wild and beautiful wilderness called the Boundary Waters Canoe Area—a large undisturbed area of granite rock, pine trees, blue waters, loons, and wolves. Not surprisingly, a number of my students had at one time visited there. And many of them mentioned experiences in nature—a star-filled night, or a glorious day canoeing, or sitting around a fire at night—when they felt a pervasive sense of peace and tranquility. Some mentioned other experiences—being present at the birth of their child, or at the death of a loved one. And some had that uplifting peaceful experience during a musical or artistic performance. As my students taught me, there are many different ways to experience the presence of a benevolent and compassionate transcendence:

- a beautiful experience in nature
- a powerful love relationship
- the birth of a child
- the spontaneous joy of a child at play
- the death of a loved one
- the elevating experience of good music
- very simple pleasures in life, like a meaningful meal with friends

Naturally, there were always a few students who could not initially identify any transcendent experience in their lives. But, as they listened to other students tell their stories, they had an opportunity to understand how others felt and to re-conceptualize some of their own personal experiences. In order to do that, they had to begin to appreciate the validity of their own feelings, intuitions, and sensory perceptions. And in that regard, a little brain science helped me understand my role as a teacher.

It is obvious, to anyone familiar with education, that academia it is primarily concerned with teaching thinking skills of an objective nature—linear skills like reasoning, mathematics, logic, and the scientific method. Those skills of sense-making are primarily a function of our left hemisphere. And academia is the home of left-brain dominance. The right hemisphere, on the other hand, processes and makes sense of more physical sensory inputs (smell, sight, and so on), as well as a variety of our emotional feelings. Thus, it is natural that educated people, being schooled in left-brain skills, have come to distrust experiences they cannot make sense of through objective reasoning. Now, *if* there is a transcendent force it is obviously wise enough to address both sides of our brain. However, when many of the clues to the Transcendent may be given to us in experiences of deep feeling, awe, and mystery, if we are relying primarily on our left brain, we will probably miss a lot of communications from Ultimate Reality.

Brain scientist Jill Bolte Taylor, Ph.D., reminds us of the brain's great talent as a seek-and-find instrument. The brain is "designed to focus on whatever we are looking for. If I seek red in the world then I will find it everywhere. Perhaps just a little at the beginning, but the longer I stay focused on looking for red . . . I will see it everywhere."[14] The big challenge in teaching spirituality is to help students take off the blinders that prevent them from "seeing red" and to create an atmosphere in which their feelings and intuitions of the Transcendent can be explored, validated and critiqued.

The exact setting of a transcendent experience is not as important as are the feelings of peace, well-being, and wonder that accompany it. The experience can be as awe-inspiring as viewing a meteor shower on an August night, or as simple as watching a child at play. Take a few quiet moments to think about a time in your life when you have experienced transcendence—a powerful, peaceful, life-affirming experience that was a clear indication of something greater than you and your everyday concerns. Hold that experience in your mind and heart as we begin to explore some of the spiritual commonalities from different wisdom traditions. Hopefully you will find connections between your own experiences and the following five themes that I believe characterize all Western spiritual traditions.

Transcendence and immanence

Benevolence and compassion

Mystery and paradox

Grace and letting go

Community

### Transcendence and immanence

As the conference at Snowmass, Colorado, affirmed, all the great spiritual traditions agree on the existence of an Ultimate Reality that goes far beyond anything we can see or know in the material world. The Transcendent does, in fact, transcend, or go beyond, our limited human capabilities to comprehend. There is a numinous or ethereal quality to the Transcendent. Still, this experience is not completely foreign or strange to us. It is also immanent and present. In the words of theologian Sallie McFague,

> ...God is not present to us in just one place...but in and through all bodies, the bodies of the sun and the moon, trees, rivers, animals and people.[15]

The paradox is that Ultimate Reality is both present to us, and beyond us, *at the same time*. Transcendence and immanence are not a dualistic pair of either/or, but a unity. The key is learning to recognize, or discern, transcendence and immanence in their common everyday forms—seeing Ultimate Reality in a wildflower, and seeing the wildflower as part of Ultimate Reality.

Many of us grew up with an overwhelmingly transcendent image of a god. I still remember, from my youth, Cecile B. DeMille's fantastic scenes from the movie *The Ten Commandments*: the walls of water standing on either side as Moses led the Israelites through the Red Sea; the power and fury of lightning engraving the Ten Commandments on a rock tablet that Moses would give to his people. Maybe you have similar images of an all-powerful god working stupendous miracles. Now power and majesty *are* important expressions of transcendence, and all spiritual traditions reference awe and majesty as "markers" of a transcendent experience; but they also give credence to the "still small voice" we often hear in our hearts. What the spiritual traditions convey to us is not only the power and majesty of the Transcendent (infinite), but also the immanent (finite) presence of an Ultimate Reality in our lives and the everyday material world. That is the great paradox: God is both infinite and finite at the same time!

To be honest, I would say that the vast majority of my own personal experiences with a Higher Power have been of an immanent and subtle nature—a conversation with a friend, a backyard visit from a songbird, a good meal, the touch of a loved one. Once in a blue moon, I have a more direct experience of a powerful encounter with a transcendent god. But most of my spiritual experiences are of a quieter, calmer nature that make me aware of the Infinite in ways difficult to put into words.

Black Elk, a spiritual leader of the Lakota Sioux, describes the sweat lodge ritual in which the transcendent elders of the community are "invited" into the ceremony. And he speaks not only metaphorically but of the very real presence of the elders in the granite rocks heated for the lodge. In Black Elk's own words, Wakan-Tanka is both "within all things" and "above all things."[16] This unity of spirit and matter (transcendence and immanence) is a common theme in much Lakota tradition.

Even more dramatically, the Sufi poets Jellaludin Rumi and Hafiz speak of the unity of the infinite Friend and our finite selves. A central theme in Sufi thought is our union with the Divine—that at our deepest, most essential level, we find God not to be separate from us. Just another spiritual paradox. Hafiz conveys that unity with the Divine in this poem:

> At some point your relationship with God will become like this:
> Next time you meet him in the forest or on a crowded city
> street there won't be any "Leaving." That is, God will climb
> into your pocket. You will simply just take yourself along![17]

**Benevolence and compassion**

The primary Western spiritual traditions all strongly affirm that our human experience with Ultimate Reality is, for the most part, affirming and loving. Certainly the Jewish scriptures provide evidence for a wrathful and jealous god, but the primary story in the Torah is that of a growing relationship between a loving god and his rebellious people, not the whims of an angry and punishing god. Of course scriptural references can be used to support and justify just about anything. Indeed, Christians from some denominations and/or sects often use quotations from scripture to make the case for a god of wrath and punishment. Within the Jewish and Christian religious scriptures, one can find justification for, and examples of, a loving and compassionate god and a god of wrath, death, and destruction. But the literatures of spirituality of both of these faiths are fairly consistent in affirming a benevolent loving God.

The same use of scripture to portray an angry god in the Islamic *Qur'an* (*Koran*) has been practiced by Al-qaeda and other terrorist groups to justify their activities. Ironically, the two words most frequently used in Islam to reference God or Allah, at the beginning of prayer and at the start of each *sura* (chapter in the *Qur'an*), are merciful and compassionate. "*Bismillah ir rahman ir rahim*" (In the name of Allah the Most Merciful Most Compassionate). Sadly, as with the Jewish and Christian scriptures, readers can find justification for war and destruction in the *Qur'an*. But, when one moves from the *religious texts* to the mystical *spiritual literatures* of Sufism, we find a consistent portrayal of a benevolent and compassionate Transcendent.

Jelaluddin Rumi, a twelfth century Sufi mystic from what is now Afghanistan, is probably one of the most widely read poets in the United States today. His work, translated by Coleman Barks, is not only accessible but almost irresistible. Rumi uses a number of names and/or metaphors when referring to the Transcendent. Most often he talks about the Friend or the Beloved. And, as you read the poetry of Rumi and Hafiz, you have an overwhelming sense of the Friend's compassion and benevolence.

The Lakota oral tradition often speaks of the Great Spirit, or Wakan-Tanka, in terms of a compassionate father and his love for his children. And the children of Wakan-Tanka include not just humankind, but all forms of life and nonsentient existence. Similarly, the Jewish scriptures, especially some of the *Psalms*, often refer to Yahweh's love for His people in terms of a mother loving her child, or a bird sheltering its young under its wings. The Transcendent takes different forms and names in these spiritual traditions, but one feels they all seem to affirm the same benevolent and loving Force.

But, for the present, don't be too concerned about names, images, or metaphors. What's more important is recognizing that you have had some personal experience of benevolence and love. One of my favorite stories, from years in 12-Step programs, is a testimony from a friend struggling to find a new image of a Higher Power. After telling me that she still wasn't sure she believed in God, she added, "But I just know that there is some thing, or some power, somewhere in the universe, that wants good for me." Some power, somewhere in the universe, that wants good for me. I love that. No need for names. She came to believe in a benevolent Higher Power because she had personally experienced its compassion.

It would be unfair to leave this discussion of Ultimate Reality without acknowledging that not all encounters with the Transcendent are warm and nurturing. One's Higher Power is not simply a smiley-faced grandfather or a warm celestial puppy. There are times when our experience with the Transcendent overwhelms us with awe, or shakes us to the core, perhaps because at times it is necessary to get our attention. But there is a big difference between shaking us and punishing us. In my reading of the various spiritual traditions, I find little, if any, evidence, for a wrathful, punishing Higher Power. True, we all suffer, but our suffering is most often attributed to our own poor choices, or our distance from God, rather than to God's punishment. But there will be times when we all receive a not-so-gentle wake-up call from Ultimate Reality. Hafiz doesn't beat around the bush.

> Love wants to reach out and manhandle us
> Break all our teacup talk of God . . .
> The Beloved sometimes wants
> To do us a great favor:
> Hold us upside down
> And shake all the nonsense out.[18]
>
> Hafiz, "Tired of Speaking Sweetly"

Just know that the motivation behind the wake-up and shake-up are compassion and benevolence.

### Mystery and paradox

There are, at least on a rational level, seemingly irreconcilable paradoxical elements in all the great spiritual traditions. Christianity contends Jesus was, at the same time, God and human, and that one has to die in order to live. The consensus of all the different religions at the Snowmass conference was that Ultimate Reality is, at the same time, both finite and infinite. Then there is the paradox of human free will and an all-powerful transcendent. In some strains of Islam, it is assumed the script of life has already been written. But at the same time, we make choices. In Rumi's words, we are both free to choose, and yet "compelled."

> Love, tell me an incident now that will clarify this mystery of how
> we act freely, and are yet compelled.[19]

16

Perhaps all the great truths are paradoxical in nature. But again, paradoxes only really make sense once we have lived them. Anyone who has been in an intimate relationship knows that the tighter you hold on to someone, the more at risk you are of losing that person. The contradiction is that sometimes, in order to keep a relationship, you have to let go. Another great paradox, from the 12-Step's philosophy, is that only after we admit we are powerless can we actually begin to exercise more control over of our lives.

In addition to mind-twisting paradoxes, there are mysterious aspects of the Transcendent that can confound us and that we may need help to understand. In *The Sacred Pipe*, the great Lakota spiritual leader Black Elk describes seven rites, or rituals, that highlight this element of mystery. One of the most powerful rituals, the sun dance, drives participants to and beyond normal human limits. In this altered state of consciousness Wakan-Tanka speaks to those who have danced sometimes for three days without food or water. Animals often deliver these messages from the Great Spirit to the dancers, and the elders must help interpret mysterious messages and visions at the ritual's completion. A similar altered state of consciousness occurs during a Lakota vision quest, in which an individual spends three days and nights (again without food or water) at a holy place (usually a mountain top) where that person experiences mysterious visions. On returning to the village the individual must have these visions interpreted by the elders. What is interesting about Lakota rituals is that the visions and messages sent to the individual are always intended for the good of the community, not merely for personal edification.

To a contemporary well-educated person, discussions of spiritual mystery can be very daunting. The concept of spiritual mystery flies in the face of so much of our rational, objective, left-brain culture, which demands empirical proof as the criterion for judging the credibility of an experience. We tend to discount or "pooh-pooh" anything that smacks of mystery. Science and empiricism are our cultural gods. Anything that cannot be explained by reason and logic is seen as suspect or pretty much worthless. In addition, it is almost un-American to admit to *not* understanding any occurrence, and especially to allow mysteries to simply be. But those who have had powerful experiences of mystery swear by their reality and the truths they reveal. As we grow more sensitive and mindful, and learn to trust our feelings and intuitions, we may discover that mystery is more present in our lives than we first imagined.

In his book *I and Thou*, the Jewish theologian and mystic Martin Buber focuses on the mysterious nature of the relationship between individuals and what Buber calls the transcendent *Thou*. (Take your time reading this one.) He argues that we experience the Thou (God) through our relationships with other humans, animals, and spiritual beings.[20] Buber's writing adds another layer of complexity to what is already paradoxical. He says that in the final analysis the personal experience we have with the Thou is indefinable. We know we have experienced something powerful, that we have been "addressed" by the transcendent Thou, but we cannot explain it to others.[21] Think of a powerful moment of transcendence, or for that matter any powerful emotional experience, you have had, and the difficulty of explaining it to even a close friend. Yet just because something is indefinable and beyond our explanation does not mean it is not real.

In the Jewish scriptures book of *Exodus*, Moses mysteriously and powerfully encounters the God of Abraham in a flaming bush on Mount Horeb. Moses is told by this god to return home and to free the Israelites from Egyptian slavery. Now this is in a time before monotheism, and Moses still believes that there are many gods. Before Moses comes down from the mountain he quite naturally asks this god, who shall he say is sending him to free his people? In other words, Moses asks for this god's name, which is equivalent to asking for God's nature. Are you a god of the mountains? of the sea? of another people? of the Chaldeans? God responds tersely, "I am Who I am," or, as others translate, "I will be Who I will be."[22] In other words, "Moses, it is not your business to know God's nature. It is enough to know *I am* the one and only God, and that I seek the freedom of my people from slavery in Egypt." Moses' attempt to plumb the nature of God's mysterious identity fails, and he must proceed on faith, and simply trust in the validity of his experience with the burning bush.

As a friend of mine, a Sufi teacher, likes to say, "In spiritual matters, the mind can only take you so far. It is simply not bright enough to fully grasp the Truth."[23] I have been a member of 12-Step groups for over thirty years. The Second Step is often a real sticking point for newcomers. It reads, "Came to believe that a power greater than ourselves could restore us to sanity." After admitting in Step One that our lives are out of control—as a result of overindulgence in drugs, drink, sex, overeating, work addiction—we are asked to trust in, and turn our out-of-control lives over to, the care of a benevolent Higher Power, of our own understanding. Now, I think it is fair to say that most addicted persons do not score high on the scale of trusting anyone, let alone God or a Higher Power. The answer to the dilemma is both simple and extremely difficult. Surrender! We have to let go of our preconceived ideas of God and be willing to explore alternatives. There is an old slogan that is both very wise and, at first, very difficult to comprehend, "Let go and let God." The spiritual traditions we are considering all have a similar message—the futility of trying to fully understand, or make rational sense of, the Ultimate Reality—the need to let go.

Sometimes it is easier to say what the Transcendent is not than to say what it is. The beginning of Rumi's poem "This We Have Now" conveys both the transcendence and mystery of the Friend. Here Rumi is commenting on the ecstatic experience Sufis have after a night of dedicated prayer and dancing.

> This we have now is not imagination.
>    This is not grief or joy.
>    Not a judging state or an elation or sadness
> Those come and go.
> This is the presence that doesn't.[24]

For Sufis, Ultimate Reality is the presence that does not come and go. It is the mysterious presence that is eternal and remains.

### Grace and letting go

A common theme in almost all spiritual traditions, Eastern and Western, is the necessity of letting go of the ego. One of my favorite posters shows a small kitten desperately hanging on to the end of a large rope. It reads, "When you get to the end of your rope . . . let go!" The sticking point is trust. We need to begin to trust in something bigger than ourselves, in something larger than our own ego. Now trusting and letting go are two character traits that go against our cultural identity as Americans: fighting the good fight, sticking it out till the end, remaining bloodied but unbowed. In our culture giving up or letting go are seen as weaknesses rather than strengths. We fight like hell to hold onto old hurts and grudges, and even to old loves. As a dear friend once told me, "Everything I have ever let go of has my claw marks all over it."

As long as we are on our own turf we feel comfortable and secure. When we let go and step out of our comfort zone, we usually experience fear. Yet stepping out, letting go, and surrendering are central points of growth in all spiritual traditions. Only then can we experience the release and freedom of *grace*. On a physical level grace is that immense sigh of relief that sometimes follows a tense undertaking—a big "Whew!" or a sense of lightness and release that accompanies us through, or after, a difficult time. Grace is a powerful feeling of release or freedom, a spontaneous gift of our Higher Power. Grace is not something we earn, or create, or prove worthy of. You cannot force a relationship with whatever form, name, or image, your Transcendent takes. Similarly, you cannot, on your own, manufacture moments of grace. It is just one more facet of the spiritual life over which we have no control. And if you are fear-based, as I am, the calm release and freedom of grace may not be a familiar experience.

We spoke earlier of awesome and positive experiences of the Transcendent in nature and high points in our lives, when we felt elated and drawn out of ourselves, or had an overall sense of well-being. That is a joyous type of grace. But there are also difficult times when grace appears. Christian theologian Paul Tillich says that sometimes in the darkest moments in our life, when we feel completely broken, a wave of light breaks through, "and it is though a voice were saying 'You are accepted, accepted by that which is greater than you and the name of which you do not know. Do not ask for the name now—Do not try to do anything—Do not seek anything. Simply accept the fact the you are accepted.'"[25] I believe in my heart that this is a message we all long to hear. That we are accepted and don't have to prove anything. That we are the *Beloved* of God.

Martin Buber says that it is through grace that we experience the *Thou* (God). And there is an elusive quality to that encounter. "The Thou meets me through grace—it is not found by seeking."[26] In so many spiritual matters, we are simply not in control. True, we must make the effort to be open and available, but, in the end, we are not ultimately in charge. Something bigger than us is. We cannot manufacture or force moments of grace to appear. They are free gifts of the Spirit, and the Spirit "blows where it will."

One of the most difficult days of my life occurred fifteen years ago when my sister and I had to admit our parents to an assisted-living residence at a Presbyterian home in Florida. We had struggled the week before to pack up all the belongings they would take with them (a painful and exhausting experience in itself). The first night at our parent's new "home" my wife and I stayed over to make sure they were settled. We slept in a separate wing of the facility, well removed from my parents. The weather outside mirrored my interior state of being—thunder, lightning, and a torrential downpour. I will never know how my mother found the room we were staying in, but she did. At 2:00 a.m. she awakened me and told me that Dad had fallen out of bed and was having a heart attack. I leapt out of bed, threw on some clothes, and breathlessly followed my mother to their room in another wing of the building. We called a medical assistant and waited while he ran a few tests and assessed Dad's condition. It turned out Dad was just scared; his heart was fine. I waited with my folks for about an hour while things settled down and they finally fell asleep. Then I walked back to my room, totally exhausted, stomach tense, and scared to death about the future. Suddenly, and inexplicably, I felt as though I was almost floating down the hallway. It all happened in a flash. I can't ever remember feeling so relaxed and so confident that everything was going to be all right. All my fears vanished in an instant. To this day I cannot explain what happened, but I know it was a moment of *grace*. I returned to my bed and fell asleep immediately. Tomorrow would take care of itself.

While I could never recreate that immense feeling of release (nor would I want to relive that night), I do know that when life gets tense and overwhelming there are things we can do to make ourselves more available to moments of grace. First, and always, breathe. Breathe deeply, but first just remember to breathe. Slow down. Listening to soothing music or getting out into nature are almost always helpful. There is a grace in the natural world that helps us get things into proper perspective. While nature can be, in the words of poet Alfred Lord Tennyson, "red in tooth and claw," nature also reflects a harmony, grace, and interrelatedness that, at times, we can all recognize as a gift from a benevolent Ultimate Reality. Mary Oliver, one of my favorite poets, has strong ties to the natural world. Her poem "Wild Geese" expresses the grace of nature better than any words I can pen.

### Wild Geese
You do not have to be good.
You do not have to walk on your knees
for a hundred miles through the desert, repenting.
You only have to let the soft animal of your body
love what it loves.
Tell me about despair, yours, and I will tell you mine.
Meanwhile the world goes on.
Meanwhile the sun and the clear pebbles of the rain
are moving across the landscapes,

21

over the prairies and the deep trees,
the mountains and rivers.
Meanwhile the wild geese, high in the clean blue air,
are heading home again.
Whoever you are, no matter how lonely,
the world offers itself to your imagination,
calls to you like the wild geese, harsh and exciting—
over and over announcing your place
in the family of things.[27]

And isn't that what we all long to feel, that at some point in our
life journey we have a home, a "place in the family of things"?

## Community

Issues of community and ethical living are at the core of all great
spiritual traditions. The Jewish and Christian scriptures, the *Qur'an*,
and the oral traditions of the Plains Indians are not so much concerned
about how the individual relates to the Transcendent, as how the community should relate to the Transcendent. Anthropologists and sociol-
ogists acknowledge that a central function of all religions is to provide
guidelines for human interaction. Spiritual seekers affirm the necessity
of faith as a communal undertaking. While all religious traditions make
allowance for some individuals to live more or less apart from the community (Christian hermits, Hasidic rabbis, Indian shamans, Muslim
dervishes), loners are the exception not the rule.

Those familiar with the Christian scriptures know that the bulk of
the *New Testament* is composed of the letters of Paul. Paul's letters are all
addressed to fledgling Christian communities in Rome, Corinth, Thes-
salonica, and so on. Their contents focus on how the earliest Christian
communities should live and how they should take care of one other. The
concern is communal, not individual behavior. As my old college chaplain, Bill Coffin, was fond of reminding young seminary students, the
spiritual journey is not a do-it-yourself project.[28] It is a communal venture
and we need each other's support, encouragement, and differing perceptual lenses. Together we can have a much better grasp of how things stand.
In that regard a sense of community is essential for anyone on the spiritual
journey. But we live in a time in which community has become sub-
servient to individualism. Indeed, individualism is so valued in our mod-

ern, urban, cultures that we often have to step back in time, to a foreign land or into a less dominant culture, to appreciate what real community feels like and how central it is to the life of a people.

I knew relatively nothing about Native American life and spirituality until I met with my first spiritual director, a Jesuit priest. Jim Egan had spent many years at the Rosebud Reservation with the Lakota people in South Dakota. While very clearly remaining a Roman Catholic, Jim came to appreciate the wisdom of the elders and how the Native American sense of community had been torn apart by forced missionary education of Indian children and by moving people from their homeland to foreign land—reservations. During Jim's years at Rosebud, in the 1960s, Native American pride was experiencing a rebirth. Old rituals and traditions began to resurface. Jim became immersed in, and adopted, much wisdom of the Lakota elders, even to the point of participating in the rigorous sun dance ritual. He subsequently introduced me to the writings of Black Elk, and I began to study the cultures of the Lakota and Ojibwe people who live in my home state of Minnesota. It was a fascinating and humbling experience and deepened my awareness of the centrality of community to native peoples.

In the process of becoming aware of the rich Native American traditions still alive in the Minnesota Native American community, I also came to know Amos Owen, a local Lakota spiritual leader. At one point I was honored to be invited to a sweat lodge ceremony. It is difficult to explain or communicate, but in every action that went into the preparations for the sweat, the actual ritual in the sweat lodge, and the meal and celebration afterwards, I became aware of the centrality of this ritual as a communal undertaking. No one person directed things, yet a very complex ritual took place flawlessly. No one called attention to themselves. All were treated equally; though as an outsider of sorts, I was treated with special attention and respect. Through that night of Lakota ritual, I began to sense the power of being in a truly organic community grounded in a greater Spirit.

The individualism that I had grown up with in my religious training, especially the centrality of a personal relationship with God through Jesus, is foreign to Lakota spirituality. All rituals are done to ensure *the health of the people* and to maintain the circle of life. Indeed, the circle, a symbol of communal unity, is a frequent and powerful image in Black Elk's tradition. It reflects a sense of organic wholeness that connects

Lakota rituals with life in general. Little, if any, separation seems to exist between Lakota spirituality and everyday life. Indeed, the very concept of religion is foreign to the Lakota. Spirit and nature are united in a gracious harmony. The rituals of the sacred pipe reflect the Great Spirit's desire for all His children to live in peace and harmony. When asked "Who are you?" most often Native Americans will respond with the name of their tribe. One's individuality is rooted in the community. And community is rooted in a common organic understanding that the Spirit pervades every element of life.

### Unity within differences—the many-faceted God

Because each of us has different experiences with Ultimate Reality, no one individual grasps the whole picture. One ancient story most of us know illustrates the paradox of unity midst difference. Six blind men are asked to describe what an elephant is like. However, each man is allowed to touch only one part of the elephant. The first has his hand on the elephant's ear and says the elephant is very much like a large thick palm leaf. Another has his arms wrapped around the elephant's leg and says it is much like the trunk of a tree. The third man is touching the elephant's side and likens it to the wall of a large house. The fourth man has grabbed the elephant's tail and says an elephant is like a piece of rope. The fifth man has hold of the elephant's trunk and says an elephant is like a large, powerful snake. The last man grasps the elephant's tusk and says an elephant is like a long, thick spear.

We can learn a number of lessons from this story. First, while each person in the story has some sense of what an elephant is like, no one individual really "sees" the whole picture. Second, if they put all their stories together, they might have a better idea of what an elephant is truly like. And, perhaps most importantly, even though each individual had a different impression of the elephant, they were all holding on to the same elephant.

The same is true of the different spiritual traditions we have been considering, which is why entertaining alternative points of view can be so enlightening. Given the nature of transcendence, its elusive qualities, and the limits of reason to understand it, we need to talk more with one another and to appreciate other spiritual ceremonies, rituals, and perspectives in order to get a better handle on this elusive, transcendent "Elephant."

Another lesson from the six blind men is an appreciation of their (and our) individual limitations. The different images that the blind men saw are not unlike the different reflections from a diamond crystal. Every turn of the stone reflects a different facet. Yet, the same stone reflects that light so differently. This crystal image helps me to think of the multi-faceted nature of Ultimate Reality. Just because different spiritual traditions envision the Transcendent differently does not mean they are not considering the same Ultimate Reality. But recognizing and honoring different facets of the Divine calls for humility on our part. And I know that it's not easy for me to admit that my perceptions are not always right on target. In spiritual matters, however, it makes sense to approach the Transcendent with respect, humility, and an appreciation for the validity of perspectives other than our own.

Though the traditions we have been exploring most often use human or anthropomorphic references to the Divine, the deeper one digs into spiritual matters, the more one realizes that human images represent a limited number of facets of Ultimate Reality. In Western culture, a preponderance of human images and metaphors for the Transcendent is inevitable. For many it is much easier to relate to a mother, father, or Rumi's concept of a Friend, than it is to feel personally close to a benevolent universal force. Still, it would be wrong to leave this discussion of the Transcendent without admitting the limitations of human images of God.

Many of my friends describe their Higher Power in impersonal terms—not that different from my friend who said she just knew there was "some power, somewhere, that wanted good for her." A number of years ago George Lucas introduced moviegoers to the *Star Wars* saga. "Long, long ago in a galaxy far away . . ." The story, characters, and ideas behind the first *Star Wars* films held immense attraction not only for Americans but for an international audience as well. Part of that attraction, according to anthropologist Joseph Campbell, was Lucas's portrayal of the Force as an impersonal source of wisdom and goodness.[29] Depersonalizing the Transcendent and calling it the Force clearly resonated with many folks' own life experiences. For them it was easier to talk about a transcendent force than to use god-language or human metaphors. The fact that this impersonal image of Ultimate Reality grabbed the imagination of so many people perhaps validates the unifying facets of the Transcendent many of us have experienced in nature, music, art, theater, and even in love-making.

For many of us, it is all too easy to conceptualize the Transcendent in anthropomorphic terms. Though a personal relationship with the Transcendent is central to *I and Thou*, Martin Buber also reminds us that God is not "limited to person."[30] It's our *perceptions* that are limited. We simply cannot take everything in. Even though the Jewish/ Christian scriptures are replete with anthropomorphic references to God, the faithful are also reminded, "my ways are not your ways, neither are your ways mine."[31] Though Rumi and Hafiz frequently use the Friend or the Beloved in referencing the Divine, there are many other, more differentiated, allusions to Ultimate Reality in Sufi thought. I was reminded recently, by a Native American writer, that the dominant white culture most often references the name Great Spirit, while Lakota people often refer to the Transcendent as Wakan-Tanka or the *Great Mystery or the Great Incomprehensibility*. That certainly stretches beyond human metaphor.

So, as we move on to consider the nature of human nature, let us keep in mind the limits of our own perspectives. We do not have to completely abandon our old concepts of the transcendent, but we do need to loosen our iron-clad grip on these images and humbly acknowledge that none of us "sees" Ultimate Reality assuredly and with clarity. And remember Rumi's warning about when we finally come face-to-face with the Truth, how we will keep repeating again and again . . .

"This is certainly not like we thought it was."

**Exercise #2 How you presently envision the transcendent**

In this chapter we used a number of different names and/or images for God or the Transcendent. Take a brief look at what you wrote in Exercise #1. Now take some time to write down, or draw, how you presently image the Transcendent. What words, images, feelings, metaphors do you find most helpful, as an adult, to describe Ultimate Reality.

# Chapter 3

# The Nature of the Human
# Condition

*People are no damn good!*

Anonymous

*O God help me to believe the truth about myself—*
*no matter how beautiful it is.*

Macrina Wiederker

W hat to say about human nature? One might think that descriptions of the human condition would be less problematic
than the paradoxes surrounding the nature of the Transcendent. But such is not the case. It seems every age sets forth new models
attempting to explain the complexities of human behavior: Plato, Freud,
Marx, Darwin, cognitive science, even computer models. Contemporary
academic models also abound from anthropology, philosophy, biology,
and psychology. Models of human nature from these disciplines can
greatly enrich our perspective. However, for purposes of our consideration, we will focus on descriptions of the human condition which pre-
sume the existence of a benevolent transcendent force. Some of these
are old and venerable, while others are modern; and there are paradoxical elements within these views. The views that follow may, at first,
seem disparate and disconnected, but there are strikingly similar themes.
Hopefully they can provide a breath of fresh air and open space to consider alternative images of the Transcendent.

The general assumptions we make with regard to human nature say
volumes about how we think of ourselves. Any individual who believes that
people are basically "no damn good," passes judgment on himself as well.
One's view of human nature also says much regarding one's concept of God
or Ultimate Reality. A number of my friends came of age in the 1950s and
1960s and now consider themselves "recovering Catholics." Most of them

27

grew up under parochial Roman Catholic education. One word summarizes the basic view of human nature they learned as children—sinner. No need for a recitation of horror stories about Sister Mary the Strict. Catholics are not alone. A number of contemporary Christian denominations and sects hold similar assessments of human nature, that is, that we are conceived and born in original sin. Not a very happy state of affairs.

If the primary lens through which I view myself is that of sinner, then my god must have a lot to do with setting the ground rules and meting out appropriate punishments. But if we are uncomfortable with this model of a punishing god, and believe that Ultimate Reality is essentially benevolent, we must still struggle with the paradox of a benevolent Transcendent and all the bad things that continue to happen to good people. All the views we will consider in this chapter affirm that there is, somehow, somewhere a benevolent Force. However, they each take a different approach regarding the nature of human nature. It will be interesting to note that, though each of these views is grounded in *religious/spiritual* roots, they also reflect amazing congruity with some contemporary secular views of human development.

### Filling the void

The seventeenth-century Frenchman Blaise Pascal was a man of many talents: physicist, mathematician, Catholic philosopher, inventor, and writer. In his philosophic treatise, *Pensées*, he offered a simple and concise analysis I have found very helpful in making sense of the human condition. Initially what Pascal says may sound a little depressing, but if we explore its consequences, his image offers a powerful insight to the relationship between human beings and Ultimate Reality. Pascal believed human beings were created by a transcendent god, but he also believed there is in each of us an abyss, or void, that can only be filled by that god.[32] In other words, without the presence of God, human nature is incomplete. Pascal also believed that human beings were created with free will, which means we have choices to make with regard to how we fill our void.

In my spirituality classes we called Pascal's analysis the "hole-in-the-soul" theory of human nature. At first glance this approach seems really unfair. If there is a benevolent Creator, as Pascal believed, why were we created with an emptiness that only that Higher Power could fill? It is not an easy question to answer. One possible answer to why we are born with such a void is that the Transcendent wants to remind us of the insubstantiality of much of the material world and the limits of our own powers. If the world and all its goods cannot satisfy our emptiness, then we must look elsewhere, toward a transcendent source. This point alone helps me reassess my childhood image of a totally self-sufficient, all-powerful deity.

Images that portray the Divine as self-sufficient and all-powerful leave little room for a personal relationship, other than total dependence on and/or fear of God. Pascal's analysis suggests other alternatives. Might it be that a benevolent Creator actually cares for us and wants to be in relationship with us? Is it possible that the Transcendent is longing for our friendship? That would be a very different way of thinking about God than most of us have ever considered.

In that regard, a Jewish Rabbinic tale is instructive. Rebbe Barukh of Medzebozh was talking one day to his grandson Yehiel. He explained, "God too is unhappy; God is hiding and no one is looking for Him. Do you understand, Yehiel? God is hiding and we are not even searching for Him."[33] It's like the old game of hide-and-seek. And the rabbi suggests how sad our Higher Power must feel knowing that we are not even looking for Her. Is it possible that God is lonely and unhappy without our companionship? If we trace out the implications of Pascal's image of human incompleteness we can begin to envision a personal relationship with a Higher Power that offers more mutuality and affirmation than one grounded in fear. Yet, at the same time, this is a relationship we need to pursue seriously in order to become fully human.

As a metaphor, the image of each of us having a void in our lives—a hole in our soul—seems to resonate with so much of life's experiences of emptiness, loneliness, incompleteness, anxiety, and despair. It's also fascinating how closely Pascal's seventeenth-century observation mirrors the insights of modern psychology, anthropology, and brain science, which also acknowledge that *Homo sapiens* is an incomplete animal.

The growth of different developmental models of human personality in the mid-twentieth century (from Abraham Maslow, Jean Piaget, Carol Gilligan, William Perry, Lawrence Kohlberg) all paint pictures of human beings as incomplete at birth and developing, through certain stages, toward adulthood (full humanness). The essential development that occurs in these stages is that we learn from other human beings and the environment. Little, if any, of our development is hard-wired into us as it is into simpler life forms. So, without love, nurture, and a variety of forms of so-cialization, we are really only human beings in a biological sense.

As every parent knows, an infant's brain progresses along develop-mental lines—first crawling, then walking, then talking. The proper wiring of the human brain depends on an orderly progression of physical/mental growth and on emotional nurturance and exposure to a variety of learning stimuli. We only truly become human through a long complex process of nurture and socialization. No one would expect a newborn child to survive without human interaction and affection. Yet sadly, there have been enough horrific, real-life examples of children locked away in attics or cel-lars—with little if any human interaction or affection—that bear out the truth of our human incompleteness. These almost feral children may be biologically *Homo sapiens* but, without human affection and encourage-ment, they have little hope of ever reaching their human potential.

In my thirty years of work in 12-Step programs I have also found this metaphor of a void in one's soul helpful in understanding addic-tion. In the first of the 12 Steps we admit that our lives are out of control due to some over-reliance on, or addiction to, alcohol, drugs, sex, over-eating, work, or concern with the emotional lives of others (co-depen-dency). In the second step we come to believe there is a benevolent Higher Power that cares for us and wants to restore us to sanity. From Pascal's perspective, we can think of any addictive behavior as an attempt to satisfy the emptiness in our lives with something material and tran-sient. And how desperately some of us have tried to fill that void!

I am not sure the creators of the 12 Steps ever read Blaise Pascal, but their recovery model makes a similar assumption, that our lives will probably not go well for us without a relationship with a benevolent Higher Power. This echoes the wisdom of the spiritual leaders at Snow-mass, who all agreed that "As long as the human condition is experi-enced as separate from Ultimate Reality, it is subject to ignorance and illusion, weakness, and suffering."[34] Indeed, the major task in 12-Step recovery is coming to know one's Higher Power and trusting that Power cares for you and wants to *restore* you to wholeness. It's interesting and a positive statement on human nature that the founders of the 12 Steps used the word restore. This presumes that we were not born insane or defective, but need help recovering our better selves. I find it more help-ful to think of myself as in need of being restored to sanity, or in Pascal's image, being incomplete without God, rather than thinking of myself as born innately bad or sinful. Somehow the image of incompleteness feels better, and less shaming, than the image of being inherently defective. This does not excuse the fact we all make mistakes, and sometimes do terrible things. Bad choices, however, may be due to a misuse of our free will, rather than an essential defect in our nature.

In any case, Pascal's metaphor of incompleteness is simply that, a metaphor—but a metaphor that engages us in thinking about the nature of our relationship with the Transcendent. Perhaps it is also suggests a means by which we can begin to make sense of the longing for wholeness that seems so present in every human heart. The arts as well as the sciences attest to the central need for affection and nurture to achieve well-being. If loneliness, fear, and anxiety are all a natural part of the human condition, and not aberrant states of being, then perhaps Pascal is on to something by portraying human nature as somehow incomplete and unfulfilled without help from a benevolent Force.

## The Sufis and longing for the Friend

To those not familiar with Sufi thought, I commend Kabir Edmund Helminski's book *Living Presence: A Sufi Way to Mindfulness and the Essential Self*. Sufism is a form of mysticism that originally developed in the context of Islam. As with other traditions we have considered, Sufis believe in the existence of one benevolent Ultimate Reality. What is unique about Sufism, as distinct from Pascal, is its emphasis on the unity of human nature with the Divine. For Sufis the main human problem is not that we are incomplete, but that we have forgotten our unity with Ultimate Reality and think of ourselves as separate from it.

This forgetfulness of our true essence is a natural part of human life, and not a defect in our human nature. It simply is. Our forgetfulness of God is exacerbated by modern materialistic culture and what Helminski calls "the tyranny of ego."[35] There are so many other materialistic "gods" in modern life that we have forgotten our essential, or *true self*, and its unity with Ultimate Reality. Instead we create a *false self*, a personality that focuses on our gender, race, occupation, physical attributes, and socio-economic standing. We are proud of, and become obsessed with, our uniqueness as individuals. Helminski writes,

31

In our obsession with our false selves, in turning our backs on God, we have lost our essential Self. . . . In forgetting God, we have forgotten ourselves.[36]

Sufis regularly engage in a practice called *ziker*, or intentionally remembering one's connection to the Divine. In and through *ziker* we rediscover our essential, or true self, which is already one with the Transcendent. This poses quite a challenge for the uninitiated. "You mean I am God?" No! Sufis do not believe we are identical with God, but, metaphorically speaking, we are like differentiated shining, divine rays from Ultimate Reality. Hafiz (fourteenth century), one of the most famous Persian poets, says we are so united with the Transcendent that God says to *us* "I am made whole by your life. Each soul, each soul completes me."[37] Though I have read some Sufi philosophy/theology that attempts to explain this unity with the Divine, I find the mystical poetry of Hafiz and Rumi a more accessible and heart-felt way to make some sense of this puzzling paradox.

Jelaluddin Rumi was born in the thirteenth century, in what is now Afghanistan. A Sufi teacher, poet, and mystic of the Muslim faith, Rumi is not so much a philosopher or a theologian as a passionate practitioner of spirituality. His poems bear eloquent testimony to the loving and compassionate nature of a Higher Power, or what Rumi calls the Friend. Let me acknowledge, from the outset, that my Sufi friends would be very upset with me were I to suggest that the poetry of Rumi is the primary window through which to view Sufism. Sufism is much broader and more complex than that. But Rumi's poetry sings with a powerful human song of longing I find irresistible. And his understanding of human nature clearly resonates with the wisdom of the other spiritual traditions we are considering.

A major theme in Rumi's poetry concerns our forgetfulness of the Friend, how we long for the Friend, and how the Friend in turn longs for us. Ultimately, though our separation from God is not real, it can feel real. In this short selection from a poem Rumi describes how an ordinary reed feels when taken from its home in the reed bed and made into a flute, but longs to return to its source. Rumi uses the reed flute as a metaphor for the human soul and the reed bed as a metaphor for God. From "The Reed Flute's Song":

Since I was cut from the reed bed,
I have made this crying sound.

32

Anyone apart from someone he loves
understands what I say.
Anyone pulled from a source
longs to go back . . .[38]

Though Rumi and Pascal are separated by four hundred years, and by two very different cultures, their insights regarding a void or emptiness in human nature and our deep longing for the Transcendent seem very compatible. The uprooted reed longs to return to its source or home. In Rumi's poetry that longing reflects a powerful yearning to return to the Friend. Indeed, the poetry of Rumi makes the case that the basis for all our longings is that we have forgotten Ultimate Reality and we long to reconnect with this loving and compassionate Force. This mirrors Pascal's analysis of how we all need to fill the emptiness in our souls. Both writers remind us of a longing for human wholeness, and an underlying need to connect with a Higher Power. The irony and the paradox is that Sufis believe we already are connected with that Ultimate Reality. But, because we have forgotten this connection, the sense of longing remains—a longing only the Transcendent can satisfy.

What are we longing for? When you talk seriously with people, we seem to share a common desire for wholeness, peace, being loved, and feeling safe and at home in the universe. But life is tough and the human condition a daily struggle. Rumi says, "Today, like every other day, we wake up empty and frightened."[39] I believe that no matter how fortunate our upbringing, we are all wounded people who feel fearful and, at times, empty. Each of us missed something in our development. And we are still longing for what we missed. We each have an emptiness that longs to be filled. Think of your life and what is missing—love, acceptance, safety, and the accompanying peace and calm that comes with the security of knowing you are loved and cared for. Our task is to recognize our longings so we can begin to connect with a Higher Power that can fulfill those longings. The good news for the Sufis—once we acknowledge our brokenness and need for the love and compassion of the Friend, we realize It has been there all along. It was not the Friend missing from the equation, but we ourselves.

**Caught between the finite and the infinite**

Reinhold Niebuhr was a liberal Protestant educator and pastor who wrote in the early to mid-1900s. He stands, without a doubt, as one of the most influential theologians of the twentieth century. His writings spanned half a century of insight and political commentary. I was introduced to Niebuhr in graduate school. And his description of the human condition helped me, for the first time in my life, begin to make sense of certain paradoxes in human nature. Niebuhr's description of the tensions inherent in the human condition are as relevant today as they were in the 1950s, and still provide an excellent lens through which to view ourselves in relation to the Transcendent.

For Niebuhr, the human condition is problematic from the outset. Humans are a strange mixture of *finite* animal and *infinite* image of the Transcendent. We are created by a benevolent God as part of a good creation. Though finite biological creatures, and thus limited, we are not flawed. In contrast to our limited finite nature, Niebuhr believes we have also been created in the image of God, with a spark of the infinite present in us, best represented by our free will. What follows summarizes some of Niebuhr's main ideas from his magnum opus, *The Nature and Destiny of Man.*[40]

Being a finite biological creature who lives and dies within the confines of this material world, conflicts with the other side of our human nature, that we are created in the image of an infinite God and possess free will. For Niebuhr the trick is to recognize and maintain a balance between our finite creatureliness and our infinite god-likeness. Our temptation, however, is to want to resolve this tug-of-war in one direction or the other. On the one hand we try to deny that we are created in the image of the Transcendent and act as if we are merely finite creatures with no divine element. The common response, "I'm only human," covers a multitude of human failings and inadequacies and can lead to justification of overindulgence in worldly matters and material goods. On the other side of the equation, we are prone to ignore our human limits and to overemphasize our infinite qualities. In simple terms, we get "too big for our britches." We become prideful and enjoy exercising power over others, or think we know best for our friends, or even haughtily imagine we are more spiritually advanced than others. In short, we act as if we were God. In either case, in Neibuhr's words, we *sin*.

Now let's pause for a moment . . . because a word like "sin" carries such heavy feeling tones. Please try to set aside any early, negative Catholic or Protestant images of men and women as being born in original sin. Niebuhr is very clear that human nature is part of God's good creation, and he uses both Hebrew and Christian scriptures to insist on that goodness. In the Genesis creation story, each day ends with "And God saw that it was good." And so it is, Niebuhr says. But if we were created good, why do we make so many bad choices?

Niebuhr was not concerned with what philosophers call "natural evil," such as, floods, volcanic eruptions, disease, tsunamis, that impact on human beings. He is thoroughly contemporary in his acceptance of most modern science. Thus he seems to assume that the natural world proceeds on its own course. A tsunami flood that kills thousands is not so much an act of God as the inevitable sorting out of the earth's tectonic plate pressures. But while Niebuhr has little to say about natural evil, he is very concerned with human evil.

If we are essentially good, as Niebuhr staunchly maintains, then why do we do bad things? A simple answer might be that through our use of free will we make bad choices. But as developmental psychologists could argue, through education and socialization, we can learn *not* to make bad choices. Niebuhr is too much of a political realist to believe that simple ignorance, or lack of education and socialization, are the causes of all our human problems. For Niebuhr, while we are not by *essence* sinners, we do inevitably sin. And that is the paradox.

Free will makes the bad use of freedom possible, but does not cause it. We cannot simply blame our free will, for that is part of our infinite nature. It is because we fail to maintain the balance between our creaturely (finite) and godly (infinite) natures that we get into trouble. We are not satisfied being both/and. Either we refuse to admit our finitude and end up pretending to be more than we are (aspiring to be godlike), or we give ourselves over to our finite nature and animal drives and lose sight of the fact that we are also created in God's image.[41] But, again, why do we find it so difficult to maintainthe balance between our finite and infinite natures? If we are essentially a part of good creation, why do we do bad things? This paradox of our dual nature—creature and divine/finite and infinite— is central to Niebuhr's understanding of human nature. It also helps him understand the reason we get into so much trouble and can do terrible things. We will explore this in more depth in the next chapter.

### The Universe as God's Body

What happens to contemporary believers of any faith when their world view, pretty much a reflection of the insights of science and reason, is so obviously at odds with world views presented in their scriptures and sacred writings? Sacred religious texts and ancient spiritual wisdom were founded on very different perspectives and assumptions about reality than those that presently exist. What happens when older images of the Divine simply seem fantastical in the light of what we currently know through the life sciences? Can we reframe our discussion of the Transcendent so that it incorporates the insights of chemistry, physics, biology, and astronomy and does not offend our intellect?

Theologian Sallie McFague, writer and former dean of Vanderbilt Divinity School, finds this dilemma fascinating. She is greatly attracted to the findings of modern biology, cosmology, and ecology. In fact, she finds the insights of the modern sciences so attractive that she feels religious believers would be foolish to ignore them. If the Transcendent is truly *transcendent*, and all discussions of the Transcendent are metaphorical or analogical in nature—at the best, approximations—why cling to old images that stretch our credibility? The world is not flat. The sun does not revolve around the earth. And is God really best imaged as a wise old man sitting on a heavenly throne? Instead, we should consider environmental ecology a reality and the insights of modern astronomy and cosmology awe-inspiring. Rather than view the sciences as enemies of theology and spirituality, McFague wants to *use* their findings to create a new theological model of the Transcendent.

She takes as her starting point—not surprising for a book penned in the 1970s—the ecological crisis that confronts us today. McFague suggests letting go of the sky-god image of an old bearded man sitting on a throne and directing all of life. Instead, she suggests using the insights of modern science to consider a new metaphor of Ultimate Reality, one that stretches beyond human anthropomorphic images to a larger, more startling, image. She asks, "What if we dared to think of our planet, and indeed the entire universe, as the body of God?"[42] How would we treat our own planet Earth if we thought of it as part of God's body? At first the suggestion sounds mind-boggling, but McFague makes a good case by insisting that since all human beings have are metaphors when it comes to envisioning the Divine, why not use a new metaphor more in line with our modern world view? She is not claiming that the universe actually *is* God's body. She is only suggesting a new model, a new image, for our consideration and asking how that image might make us feel and behave.

Although we have only images and metaphors to describe the Transcendent, they are still very important, for they help frame how we think and act. And in that regard, some metaphors are more helpful than others. McFague believes the story told by modern science of life's incredible interdependence and interrelatedness not only makes common sense but provides an exciting model for thinking about how humans might live in relation to their environment and the Transcendent.

Sallie McFague asks us to consider what she calls the modern creation story, described for us by astronomers and modern cosmologists. This story traces back more than fifteen billion years to the initial occurrence of the Big Bang. Of course secular scientists and ecologists do not see the hand of God as the initiator of the Big Bang, nor as directing billions of years of evolution on earth that eventually produced *Homo sapiens*. According to science, life came into being not because God bent down and breathed the breath of life into "man" but simply through randomness and chance. Quite understandably, modern empirical science has little room for the existence of a benevolent god. In today's dualistic parlance, one either believes in God or in evolution (that is, science). And never the twain shall meet.

While Sallie McFague believes in, and affirms the ecological relationships of interdependence and interrelatedness portrayed by the sciences, she also believes in the existence of a benevolent transcendent. However, she also wants to avoid philosophical/theological debates about God's existence as Creator and the cause of the Big Bang. She is more concerned about the ecological situation today. As she says, ". . . whatever may have been the mechanism of evolutionary history in the past," it is clear, from the negative impact humans are having on the environment, that our attention needs to be focused on *what we do with the situation*, not how we got here.[43] And she wants to use the insights of science in that endeavor because she believes that the awesomeness of the universe presents a good picture to turn to "when we try to envision divine transcendence."[44] Most of the pictures painted by modern science (with the exception of randomness) are consistent with her own religious beliefs and, she believes, represent transcendence metaphorically better than an old man in white garments sitting on a throne.

Rather than pretending we have dominion over the creatures of the earth, we need to recognize our rightful place as a creature who is, in fact, dependent on lower life forms. Three and a half billion years ago (after a billion years of cooling), life first developed in our oceans in the form of algae that began producing oxygen so that other life forms could develop. As recently (in geological time) as a million years ago, primitive human beings first walked the earth. Imagine trying to trace your family tree all the way to algae. That not only boggles the mind but gives us pause for humility and appreciation for what we often call "lower forms of life."

If we take seriously the insights of modern ecology and evolutionary theory, then human life becomes dramatically de-centered from earlier Christian and Jewish assessments. We are not only close relatives of the great apes, we are distant cousins to the first armored fish and giant prehistoric ferns. If we continue back in time, beyond the four and half billion years when earth was formed, to the Big Bang, fifteen billion years ago, we realize, as John Polkinghorn, the author of *One World: the Interaction of Science and Theology*, reminds us, "we are made of the ashes of dead stars."[45] And that provides not only a lovely metaphor to help us understand how interrelated and interdependent all life is, it is also, so far as secular science is concerned, *a fact*. We really are physically composed of "the ashes of dead stars." And all matter, everywhere in the universe, is part of a giant recycling process.

As the atoms that exploded out of the Big Bang expanded into universes, stars, and eventually planets, they began to cycle and recycle. In our own solar system, here on planet earth, the water that formed three and a half billion years ago is still present today. The earth does not create new water. The water in your body today existed three and a half billion years ago. Imagine where just one molecule of water, present in your body right now, has traveled during all those years. And where will it go when it passes out of your body? That should engender an attitude of humility and awe in each of us.

Viewing human nature as a miraculous mix of interdependence and interrelatedness provides a firm foundation and new direction for an ethic of responsibility. Sallie McFague believes we need a lot more humility and a new set of "house rules" here on planet earth.

> One of the most critical house rules we must learn is that we are not lords over the planet, but products of its processes, in fact, we are the product of a fifteen-billion-year history of the universe and a four-billion-year history of our earth.[46]

Sallie McFague offers a radically new metaphor for thinking about Ultimate Reality with her description and portrayal of the beauty and wonder of a new creation story. And the fact that this new metaphor resonates with how many of us believe the natural world actually operates perhaps provides a rich alternative to our older sky-god image.

## Human nature in relation to the transcendent

Central to our discussion in this chapter has been the assumption that there is a benevolent Ultimate Reality that helps define human nature and serves as a foundation for our personal and communal spirituality. The models of human nature presented, though all grounded in some form of transcendence, have been, of necessity, limited and selective. Other models could have been used. The intent, however, is to consider alternative images to those which have so dominated the Judeo-Christian-Islamic traditions—alternative lenses through which we can contemplate and reconceptualize our relationship with the Transcendent.

It may surprise us that these different models of human nature and spiritual traditions have so much in common. After studying Sallie McFague's *The Body of God*, I was amazed at its fundamental congruity with many Lakota images. The interrelatedness and interdependence of all life are central to the message of Black Elk, and to most Native American spiritual traditions. And it didn't take modern ecology for them to figure that out. Black Elk speaks quite naturally of birds, fish, and deer as relatives. Humans are part of the interconnected web of life, no better or worse than any aspect of Mother Earth. I again recall my first sweat lodge ritual and how strange it felt to welcome hot granite rocks into the lodge as my relatives. I could make the *stretch* of my relatedness to animals as my brothers and sisters, and could even entertain plant forms as living spirits, but never before had I considered rocks as anything other than dead (nonsentient) matter. To my Native brothers present in the sweat lodge, such interrelated and interdependent thinking was natural. It was just as true for their earlier ancestors who lived on the great plains and considered the buffalo not only a source of food, clothing and shelter, but also knew it to be their brother. And if one accepts some of the truth of modern science and cosmology's finding—that our bodies are actually composed of the ashes of dead stars—those same ancient ashes make up the substance of the granite rocks brought into the sweat lodge. Maybe the leap to radical inter-relatedness is not as far as I first imagined.

Rumi, Pascal, Black Elk, Niebuhr, and McFague all lived at different times with very different world views, yet there is much congruity among them. If life is more than this material existence, and if there is a benevolent Ultimate Reality that not only created us, but intended for us to be in relationship with Her/Him, then I much prefer imaging that relationship in terms of a longing for a Higher Power, or being incomplete without the Divine, or being a strange mix of finite and infinite, or as an interrelated part of the Transcendent, than I do imaging myself as born with some original defect or sin.

I recently ran into an old friend who used to attend our church. Ralph, who customarily had a hang-dog aura about him, looked almost radiant. He had grown up with an image of human nature steeped in original sin. And, for the first time since leaving his church of birth, Ralph had begun to affiliate with a local Christian Science congregation. He almost bubbled over in telling his story. "Do you know what they told me?" he asked breathlessly. "That I am the Beloved of God. No one *ever* said that to me before—that I am beloved by God." I teared up hearing his story. Here was a seventy-three-year- old man who for all that time had labored under the image he was primarily a sinner. And now he was told, *and it broke into his consciousness*, that he was God's Beloved. A radical change in his view of human nature and, consequently, his own self-esteem. That's how important metaphors and images of the transcendent and human nature can be. They help us define our very being.

**Exercise #3 What generalizations come to mind when you think about human nature?**

Our childhood experiences and rearing have a big influence on our individual views of human nature, and thus our self-image. A strong religious upbringing can also have a powerful impact. In any case, our personal views of human nature are rooted in our past experiences. Try to describe, as simply as possible, the view of human nature you had as a child.

How has that view changed as you have matured into an adult?

Chapter 4

# When Bad Things Happen

*The question is not:*
*How can I explain the events that occur?*
*You should ask rather: What can I make of them?*

Albert Schweitzer

Wat philosophers and theologians call "the problem of evil"
is one of the thorniest issues that plague believers of any faith,
and one that must be addressed by anyone on the spiritual
journey. Human beings are a special kind of creature—a curious combination of reason and emotion—and we demand some degree of order
and explanation for how and why things happen. Thus, for those who
believe in a compassionate and loving Transcendent, it is natural to
want to know the whys and wherefores when natural disasters kill scores
of people, or when a deranged shooter kills innocent school children.
What are we to do with the paradox that we believe God is good and
yet these terrible things happen?

For purposes of our discussion it is important to distinguish
broadly between two types of bad things—natural evil, the result of what
scientists regard as the laws of nature; and human evil, which results
from human beings in the exercise of our free will.

> Natural evil—Lightning strikes and kills two Boy Scouts camping
> in a forest.
> Human evil—A drunk driver goes off the road and kills a four-year-
> old girl playing nearby.

### Bad things in nature

Natural evil refers to occurrences in the physical world that, from
*a human perspective*, result in destruction, death, and tragedy. Examples

include violent weather patterns, genetic mutations, and shifting tectonic plates. When I first began writing this chapter, a tsunami had just struck Japan, killing thousands with its initial wave of disaster. But consider this. If human beings were not present, and directly impacted by this tidal wave, would it command our attention and be in the newspaper headlines day after day? Would we even consider it a tragedy? Similarly, lightning strikes the earth thousands of times each minute, every day of the year. Normally, when we see or hear lightning we don't ask "Why?" We accept it as a natural process in the weather cycle. We may even stand in awe of its power and beauty. But when lightning kills two young boys, those closest to them, and even complete strangers, ask "Why?" The impact on human life changes our perceptions from what was a beautiful light show of nature into a human tragedy.

It is fair to say that human beings suffer from a unique sense of ego centricity or *speciesism*. Too frequently we believe we are the highest, or most advanced, species that evolution, and/or God, produced, and, therefore, we deserve special consideration. Our expanded egos tempt us to perceive everything revolves around us, and we should, somehow, be exempt from natural disasters. Once again the expanded ego that Kabir Helminsiki, Reinhold Niebuhr, and Sallie McFague talk about, raises its ugly head. Whenever human life has been taken by some force of nature, we question why?

There need be no mysteries in this regard. Often what we call natural evil is the result of poor prior choices made by humans. It does not seem fair to implicate a Higher Power, or to shake our fist at Mother Nature, when flooding in rivers is natural, and yet humans insist on building houses, towns, and even major cities on natural flood plains. Similarly, being struck by lightning is more a case of being in the wrong place at the wrong time. Still, we demand an accounting. If Ultimate Reality is caring and compassionate, then what role does It play in these natural tragedies? At least three explanations are commonly offered.

> 1. A benevolent, all-powerful Force creates the world, which then operates on its own, on the basis of what we call natural laws. Tornadoes are a natural function of certain weather patterns. Birth defects result from random genetic mutations, but they also fuel the general process of evolution.

For those who believe in a benevolent Creator, the most common explanation for natural disasters is to absent God from the process and to view such disasters as a part of the natural order of things. Ultimate Reality remains benevolent and all-powerful but does not intervene to stop a tsunami from killing thousands. At the same time, the Transcendent does not intentionally cause these natural disasters, nor does It wish ill on the human community. These events simply demonstrate that human life is uncertain, given the way Nature works.

This perspective may offer little consolation to those directly impacted. What we consider a human tragedy occurred, and anger is still expressed because the Transcendent did not intervene. And, in this model, there is no explanation as to why the Divine did not intervene. Perhaps because we most often image the Transcendent as all-mighty and all-powerful, we assume It is behind every disaster that impacts human civilization. However, if we believe Ultimate Reality is all-powerful, then It can also let nature run its course and choose not to intervene.

So, if Ultimate Reality had no role in causing a natural disaster, and does not intervene to stop it, how does the Transcendent impact on human life after the tragedy? Those who believe in a gracious Higher Power, and have experienced personal loss and tragedy, often testify that the story does not necessarily end in tragedy, loss, and grief. Many would argue, from their experiences after such a tragedy, that a Force greater than themselves consoles, nurtures, and helps heal their suffering. They also believe human beings serve as instruments of God's love and are a big part of this consolation and healing. Natural disasters are just part of the way the world works. And when terrible natural disasters tear up the human community, a compassionate Transcendent suffers with us and works with and through us to console and heal those in pain.

2. What we think of as a natural tragedy is really for the best in the long run and part of Ultimate Reality's overall plan.

A number of religious systems, including much of traditional Judaism, Christianity, and Islam contend that the Transcendent is indeed merciful, all-powerful, and all-knowing and remains the primary cause of all that happens. What appears to us a natural tragedy is, in the long run, intended for the good. In other words, everything happens for a reason. Human perspective is just too limited to understand the final good that will result from what we perceive as a natural disaster. In short, we do not appreciate the big picture. Such a view was voiced by Pope Benedict soon after the tsunami of March 2011. In his first televised question-and-answer interview on Italy's national broadcast, Pope Benedict said, in relation to the tsunami, "This suffering was not empty, it wasn't in vain, but *behind it was a good plan*."[47]

Again, this is small consolation to the thousands who died or lost loved ones and homes, and yet we all know that good can come out of tragic situations. In the end a tsunami might be a pivotal event, awakening all the world's nations to abandon petty disagreements and thus helping to bring about a stronger, more unified human community. Or the resulting nuclear disaster from this tsunami might spur humans to invest in cleaner forms of solar and wind energy. This long-term explanation makes sense on one level, though it is hardly a consolation to those whose loved ones were killed. This same argument, of limited human understanding of God's long-term wisdom, is frequently used to rationalize human evil, as we will see in the next section.

> 3. God is benevolent and transcendent and the universe/natural world are part of a good creation. But our images of the Transcendent as an all-powerful monarch set us up to blame the Divine for any bad news that nature throws our way. Perhaps Ultimate Reality is not all-powerful and, through the gift of free will, shares power with us and needs our help (as co-creators) to do the follow-up work of grieving, healing, and consolation.

Transcendent, but not all-powerful, sounds like an oxymoron, but perhaps it is just another paradox. So much of Jewish/Christian/Islamic traditions are wrapped up in images of an omnipotent, all-powerful God who creates, directs, and is the Primary Cause of everything that happens. But again, these images are only metaphors for understanding how the Transcendent operates. If our Higher Power is all-powerful and all-knowing, then it makes sense to say that everything—good and bad—happens for a reason. However, it is quite another perspective to consider a transcendent God who is not all-powerful, who does not direct all of life, and who, through the gift of free will, *shares power* with humankind.

In this model God remains the benevolent creator of the universe, the world, and its natural laws, but is powerless to intervene in natural events. Still, this benevolent God suffers with us and can, through various means, provide strength, courage, and consolation to deal with our grief, loss, and anger. Part of the rationale for this argument is that Ultimate Reality responds to human tragedy by and through human beings as instruments of Her love and compassion. In the sixteenth century, St. Teresa of Avila reminded her followers that Christ has no hands or feet on earth; human beings do. When we act in merciful ways, we are instruments of the Transcendent. *We are* God's hands when we bind up the wounds of those injured. *We are* the feet of the Divine when we walk in a fund-raising event for women with breast cancer. In this scenario, we have to admit that life is uncertain, but that a Higher Power needs and uses human beings as instruments of Its healing and consolation.

Before dismissing the combination transcendent-but-not-all-powerful as a word-game contradiction, one final metaphor/image—consider the example of Jesus of Nazareth. Jesus certainly was not the Messiah that most Jews, or even his disciples, envisioned. They expected the Davidic kingdom to be restored by a powerful Messianic leader who would overthrow the Romans and all the enemies of the Jews. Instead, this Jesus god-man comes to earth, talks about forgiveness of enemies, and dies on a cross. So many of Jesus' parables and admonitions turn the all-powerful god metaphor upside down. "The first shall be last and the last shall be first." The compassionate example of Jesus washing his disciples' feet during the Passover meal clearly demonstrates that Jesus envisioned the Davidic kingdom as one of service. Jesus modeled servant-hood, not military victory, and, for his followers, he flipped the all-powerful God image on its head. So, as we consider new metaphors and images, let's add benevolent and power-sharing Transcendent to our repertoire of paradoxical images and metaphors. And remember how leaders like Gandhi and Martin Luther King, Jr., powerfully demonstrated the compassion and efficacy of passive resistance and nonviolent love, as opposed to combative intervention.

It is a challenge to stay on the spiritual path and believe in the reality of a compassionate transcendent Force while, at the same time, admitting that life is uncertain and that we live in a chancy world. The testimony of the great spiritual traditions is that we can live with uncertainty, endure natural tragedies and still experience the benevolence, love, and caring of a transcendent and immanent Higher Power. In the words of my old chaplain William Sloane Coffin, God may only offer us "minimum protection" but also provides "maximum support."[48]

## Bad things human beings do

Natural evil has never been as problematic to grapple with as human evil. A drunk driver kills a little girl; financial bad-boys defraud elderly people of thousands of dollars; a mother physically abuses her newborn and throws its body in a trash heap. The classic response to these, and many more instances of human evil, is to see them as the consequence of the misuse of free will. According to the Christian and Jewish traditions, human beings possess free will and simply make bad choices. But if we believe in a benevolent and loving creator, and that human beings are part of that good creation, we are still left with the question, "Why do essentially good people do such terrible things?"

In the context of a caring Transcendent, who creates us with free will, we might ask, "Why does God not intervene when we make bad choices?" This is not so much a problem when, for example, a drunk driver kills himself by running into a tree. We can say, "Well, he made some bad choices and his death was probably inevitable." But, if another driver goes off the road and, instead of dying himself, kills an innocent four-year-old, the "Why" question arises immediately. Why must the innocent die? Why didn't God intervene and sweep that child up from the path of the car's path? We can argue that these terrible happenings are the cost of free will, but that does not relieve our pain, our suffering, or our need for explanations. "Why?" is the question the child's parents are asking. In what follows we consider four different models that grapple with the issue of why human beings misuse their free will and make bad choices, in relationship to a benevolent Transcendent.

> 1. Bad choices are simply the result of learned behavior or ignorance and the *misuse of free* will.

In considering the case of a drunk driver killing an innocent child, we might come to understand the cause of that person's drunkenness as rooted in his own alcoholism. Thus, the death of the child was not the intentional result of this man's action, but an almost inevitable accident, given the driver's history of alcoholism and perhaps his rearing and/or socialization. Today we have come to understand a lot about human learning and family dynamics. As incomplete animals we learn how to behave. We learn to be good. We learn to be bad. We can also learn to be irresponsible. We make choices every minute of every day.

But they are seldom random. Some of our patterns of behavior are shaped by our genetic inheritance. But to a larger extent, our behavior is a function of our rearing, socialization, and education.

Born as incomplete animals, we come into life pretty much a blank slate, ready to be written on by all of life's experiences. For this reason, both secular and religious education have been seen as roads to improvement and enlightenment. Without education things often go awry. The woman who leaves her young child in a locked car on a hot day did not intend for her child to die. She was simply ignorant of the consequences of her action. We can blame many human tragedies on human ignorance, failed education, lack of attention (running a red light), and randomness. If we only knew better, and paid attention, these tragedies need not have occurred, and education could have come to the rescue.

The Greek philosopher Plato believed in a transcendent source of goodness, and further, that if humans came to know that Goodness, they would lead virtuous lives. Plato's Socratic dialogue, *The Republic*, details a system of education in which (though they may fulfill different functions) every person has an opportunity to lead a virtuous life. Americans share much of this optimistic view of human nature. We believe education is the key to a better life, and for many it is. But, if learning and virtue were synonymous, with more education shouldn't we expect a steady improvement in the human condition—fewer wars and murders, less violence and poverty?

Is mere ignorance of the Good sufficient explanation for the magnitude of the evil of the Holocaust? Can we blame the Holocaust on Hitler's inadequate education, or his family's dynamics? In recent years, ironically (and in contradiction to Plato's theory of education for virtue), some of the worst villains of financial scandals have degrees from Harvard and Yale. Why isn't a good education a sufficient guarantor against people doing bad things?

2. Bad choices are the result of a *basic defect in human nature.*

The image of humankind born under original sin is a classic Jewish/Christian model used to explain why we make bad choices. The Genesis story of our first rebellion in the Garden of Eden tells us that as a result of that first act of disobedience—eating from the tree of the knowledge of good and evil—the die was cast for all of humanity. Henceforth, we are all born as sinners, and something inherent in us wants to rebel against the Divine. We can lead more or less virtuous lives through prayer, communal worship, and other spiritual practices, but fundamentally we remain sinners, and only God can redeem us.

For thousands of years, the concept of original sin has been used, particularly by Christians, to explain the paradox of why human beings, created in the image of a benevolent and compassionate Ultimate Reality, continue to make bad choices. The seeds of our own destruction, and violence against others, are planted within us through original sin. In this model we are not essentially evil, because we were created out of the goodness of the Transcendent. But, in addition to our goodness, we have been branded with original sin. And, when this is combined with free will, we want to rebel against our Higher Power. Still the paradox remains in the co-existence of these two opposed natures—image of God and sinner. Why were we destined to the curse of original sin? Why does the Divine not intervene when through our sinfulness we injure others?

> 3. Bad choices are in part due to the existence of an *external force of evil*, opposed to the goodness of God.

In this model, free will is again seen as a big part of the problem, but instead of humans being born with a defect in character (that is, sin), we remain essentially good, but must deal with external forces of evil. The liberal Christian theologian Reinhold Niebuhr stands as an interpreter of this model for why we do bad things. Earlier we described Niebuhr's understanding of human nature as a strange admixture of creatureliness (finite) and god-like transcendence (infinite). These two parts of our nature are in constant tension with each other, a tension that wants to be resolved. Thus, we are tempted to resolve that tension by choosing one side or the other. We either become prideful (too god-like) or we lose ourselves in sensuality (too creaturely). In Niebuhr's words, we sin.

Thus far this scenario sounds like the previous, classical, Jewish/Christian model. But it differs in one important respect. As a liberal Protestant theologian, Niebuhr does not want to blame the bad things we do on a defect in our essence. We are not born sinners; we are born part of God's good creation. We are essentially good and possess free will. For Niebuhr, present-day and historical evils are "a corruption of human freedom."[49] While it is inevitable that we will sin, sin or evil is not an essential part of human nature. So how to resolve this paradox? Why do we inevitably sin? Enter an external evil force—the devil.

Now let's pause again . . . Remember when we discuss the transcendent Good, we are always speaking metaphorically. The same is true when considering an external source of evil. It is not necessary to conjure up thirteenth-century images of a horrific devil (always red), with horns, a long tail, and usually accompanied by a pitchfork for prodding us along on our way to Hell. Niebuhr spends precious little time in his writing trying to describe the nature of this evil force. He is not interested in its specific size, shape, or makeup. But, having lived through the horrors of World War II, and not seduced by the optimism of education as a cure-all, Niebuhr does believe there is evil afoot and sees the "devil" as a meaningful *symbol*.

According to Christian mythology, even the devil was not created as evil. Niebuhr, speaking symbolically and mythologically, says, "The devil is a fallen angel, a corruption of something good . . ." an angel who overstepped his bounds and tried to ascend to become equal with God.[50] It is clear that, for Niebuhr, this force of evil is never co-equal with God but is certainly powerful enough to lead human beings astray. And, for Niebuhr, evil is much more subtle than the horrific images often portrayed in movies. The very few times we read of a devil in Niebuhr's theology, he describes it more as a power or force that tempts us to either overstep our creaturely limits and get too big for our britches, or to sink into animal sensuality and deny the image of God in which we are created. Perhaps a better image (than a horrific devil) is an allusion often used by the early desert hermits who referred to the devil as the Father of Lies, a master illusionist.

There is no full-blown demonology in the Bible, or in Niebuhr's theology. However, in the Hebrew scripture's *Genesis*, an evil force appears through the representation of the serpent (paradoxically a part of God's original good creation) tempting Eve and Adam to overstep the bounds set by God not to eat of the tree of the knowledge of good and evil. The Hebrew scriptures are replete with examples of both individual and communal rebellion against God's goodness, though the image of a devil is not prevalent. In the Christian scriptures, however, the devil plays a key role in Jesus' temptation in the desert and pops up from time to time as demons in some healing stories and the final passion story. It's clear that Jesus believed there was an evil force, called it by name—Satan—and urged his followers to resist its temptations. It seems ironic that the founder of Christianity not infrequently encountered demons and was challenged by the "devil," and yet many modern liberal Christians so easily dismiss evil as a myth.

Most Americans share a basically optimistic view of human nature, in which our problems can be solved either through therapy, medication, education, and/or the elimination of poverty. We are so sophisticated that any reference to an external evil force seems naïve and antiquated. We forget that, through human history, most western cultures have seen life as a struggle between forces of good and evil. Though their stories and images differ widely, most Native American traditions I am familiar with acknowledge the existence of evil spirits that tempt one to stray from the path of virtue. While no central evil figure or "devil" exists in Lakota traditions, the Lakota spiritual leader Black Elk, tells his people to beware of "bad spirits" that can lead them astray.[51] The culture of the Navajo people of the Southwest is replete with witches and evil "skin walkers"—different images and metaphors for the source of bad things that happen to us. Perhaps we urban sophisticates too lightly dismiss these references to evil forces most men and women throughout human history have acknowledged. A Cornish prayer as recent as 1926 reminds me that, no matter how sophisticated we seem, we still hold primal fears on dark and scary nights.

> From ghoulies and ghosties and long-legged beasties, and things
> that go bump in the night, good Lord deliver us.
> *The Cornish and West Country Litany*, 1926[52]

It takes a lot of letting go of old images to entertain this model of a Transcendent, loving Higher Power and an opposing evil force. I still have difficulty with old "devil" images, but I like the words my spiritual director uses each time we end a session with prayer. She says, in closing, ". . . and God protect Chet from all that is not You." All that is not God. That's a nice turn of phrase and an image free of pitch-forked devils.

But, even if we accept that a source of evil exists external to human nature and God's good creation, the same questions and paradoxes remain. How did this evil force come to be? Why does a benevolent Ultimate Reality permit an evil force to influence human affairs and lead us astray?

> 4. Human beings tend to think of life in terms of opposite distinctions—good and bad—and fail to see the big picture that Ultimate Reality is a *unity* that cannot be reduced to a simple dualism of good and evil.

Sufism, originally rooted in the Muslim faith, has historically taken a number of forms, yet always retaining the central theme that the Transcendent is a merciful and compassionate unity. Our mortal life and human history are but a thin skin covering this greater essential unity. What we think of as human "evil" is really, in large part, a result of our losing sight of the ultimate unity of life. While most Sufis would never deny that we often feel bad things happen, they also believe human perspective is just too limited to understand the ultimate ways of God. Sufis also contend that what we view as evil is the result of our basically unenlightened consciousness and behavior. A poem of Rumi's "The Dream That Must Be Interpreted" captures the feeling of this rationale.

> This place is a dream
> Only sleepers consider it real.
> Then death comes like dawn,
> and you wake up laughing
> at what you thought was your grief.[53]

Rumi's poetry brilliantly conveys what Sufi mysticism is all about at a feeling level. And modern Sufi interpreters provide a more rational, left-brain explanation for understanding what appears to be human evil.

Hazrat Inayat Kahn (1882-1927) was a great Sufi teacher, writer, and musician who established "The Sufi Order in the West," or Universal Sufism. Hazrat was born in India in 1882 into a well-respected family of musicians. As a young man, he became an accomplished musician of the Vina, a stringed Indian instrument, and began to tour India, but he was increasingly drawn toward the spiritual life and became a disciple of a teacher of the Chistis Sufi order. To make a long story short, as his teacher was dying, he turned to Hazrat and said, "Go to the Western world, my son, and unite East and West through the magic of your music."[54] Two years later, in September of 1910, Hazrat sailed for America. And, as they say, the rest is history. His interpretation of Sufism has profoundly shaped Sufi thought and practice in America.

Hazrat contends that one of the main problems in seeking to understand Ultimate Reality is that we have grown up learning to think in terms of opposites, to make all kinds of distinctions, but especially between good and evil. And this way of thinking is natural on our mortal journey—*natural, but not correct.* Hazrat believes such distinctions are at first necessary, for they help us make some sense of life.

> . . . it is not right to conceive of God, who is all powerful, as having another personality, an opposite power, which one calls the devil. But at the same time it would puzzle a believer who considers God to be all goodness and all beauty if he were told that Good also contains everything that is bad and evil.[55]

The error with our dualistic way of thinking is that it obscures the essential unity that lies behind all appearances. For Sufis, making distinctions like good and evil is a first step on the way to appreciating life's essential unity. The problem is that, especially in American culture, we have been so socialized to think in terms of opposites that we believe these distinctions are real. Just as images and metaphors can only take us so far in understanding the Divine, so with dualistic distinctions. In the final analysis, that is all they are—helpful distinctions. According to Sufis, the real Truth regarding Ultimate Reality is its essential goodness and unity.

For Universal Sufis, one's perspective is crucial. How we look at life determines whether we see an incident as good or evil. Sufis are urged not to worry about making these kind of distinctions because ". . . behind all life is oneness, and that wisdom lies in the understanding of that oneness."[56] Sufi mysticism is one route not only to come to understand and appreciate Ultimate Reality's unity but to living it. When we live in this unity, the apparent paradox of a good God and bad things happening dissolves. Once we understand the unity of life, we will appreciate that, in the final analysis, everything that happens is according to the will of God. In the final analysis evil is an illusion. We are confused by our limited perception, but through practices of Sufi mysticism we will come to know the unity of life. Still, we must grapple with the world of distinctions that surround us. And, although Ultimate Unity does seem to dissolve the paradox of good and evil, is not this unity a paradox in itself? Why do the distinctions of good and evil seem so real if they are but an illusion?

Thus far we have explored different models, images, and metaphors for why bad things happen—we are ignorant of the good; we are born in original sin; we are tempted by an evil Force; we don't see things clearly; nature just runs its course. Admittedly, none of these resolves the paradox in our hearts or minds. The occurrence of bad things can become an occasion for cynicism and disbelief, or an occasion for hope and a deeper belief in the benevolence of a Higher Power. The point is not so much to better understand the cause, but to consider *what we do* when confronted with tragedies in our lives.

### A close-to-home case study

In March 1996, my niece Bonnie died when her husband shot her in the chest. My family is still dealing with that tragedy. Back then, as now, it was no consolation to know that Bonnie's husband had made bad choices, was an alcoholic, and had somewhere along the way learned to abuse women physically. All that may be true, but it offered no consolation. A beautiful, innocent, young woman, a brilliant lawyer—and my loving niece—was dead.

This terrible event is fresh in our minds, for as I am writing this, Bonnie's husband has just finished serving fifteen years of his thirty-year sentence and is theoretically now eligible for parole. Anger arises fresh to the surface. And none of the foregoing assessments of human evil console my sister or our family. Anger, yes! Why didn't God prevent it? The hell with free will. If God is good, why did Bonnie die? Is forgiveness possible?

If it is difficult for me, as a loving uncle, to begin to comprehend the feelings of my sister Barbara, Bonnie's mother. Last year, fourteen years after the event, I asked my sister how she initially dealt with Bonnie's death. I could not believe her grace. To her credit, she never blamed God for her daughter's death. Her primary concern was that Bonnie's husband be found guilty and sentenced to prison where he could no longer hurt women. Anger at the perpetrator? Immense. Desire for his punishment? Yes! A challenge to her personal faith and well- being? Certainly.

Immediately after Bonnie's death, and to this day, there is surprisingly little consolation in exploring the whys and wherefores—that is, the exact cause of this tragedy. The question remains, after the initial trauma of a tragic event, what do we do next? Grief experts say the death of one's child is more difficult to deal with than even the death of a spouse. How does my sister go on living when her child has been murdered? Where would you turn? What happens to one's relationship with a Higher Power at that point? If the Transcendent is benevolent, merciful, and compassionate, how do we access that benevolence, compassion, and love? What, if anything, can ever fill this new immense void in our lives? I do not know. I simply do not know the answers to these questions.

The questions my sister and our family face are not that different from questions and concerns each of us must confront at some point in life. Images and metaphors may help us get a partial grasp on the bad things that happen in our lives, but none of them finally answer the questions in our hearts that so want to be resolved.

Much more time could be spent wrestling with the whys and wherefores of human tragedies. But at some point we need to move beyond the question of why bad things happen and focus on what we are going to do about the situation. How do we deal with the resulting pain, loss, and sorrow? The brief quote below, delivered in a sermon by Albert Schweitzer at St. Nicholas's Church in Strasbourg, Germany, points us in that direction.

> Where shall I direct your thoughts that we may together turn sorrow, pain, and distress into peace of mind? I will give you the blessing—the peace of God that passes all understanding.
> The question is not: How can I explain the events that occur? You should ask rather: What can I make of them?
> That is the profound understanding for which we must struggle.[57]

At some point, we must realize there may never be a satisfactory explanation for why bad things happen. They simply do; as the crude old bumper sticker reminds us, "Shit Happens!" We need to move in a different direction by dealing with our loss and deepening our spiritual practice. Our heads may never understand the whys and wherefores of bad things that happen, but our hearts can mend and we can move on. And that is where the remainder of this books seeks to offer some practical help.

**Exercise #4 What do you say to yourself when something "bad" happens to you?**

Think of a past event in your life that, at the time, you considered "bad." Briefly describe how you felt at the time. How do you feel about that past event now? Where is/was the Transcendent in this event?

Did any good come out of this event?

Chapter 5

# Belief, Faith, and Doubt

*You cannot be a person of faith unless you know how to doubt.*

Thomas Merton

As stated earlier, this book is written for those of us who believe, or want to believe, in the reality of a benevolent transcendent force, whatever we may call it: God, Yahweh, Allah, Wankan- Tanka, Ultimate Reality, the Divine, the Friend, Great Mystery, the Force, and more. Though we struggle, and at times doubt in the face of bad news and personal tragedies, we persist in our belief in the goodness of a Higher Power. But what does it mean to say we believe? Is there a difference between belief and faith? And is there a role for honest doubt in the spiritual life? Once again we face the problem of words and their meanings—belief, faith, doubt. In what follows we will try to clarify, and perhaps reframe, these words, because they are so central to our spiritual journey.

## Belief

For many of us, from a variety of religious traditions, believing means agreeing with a series of statements or propositions—a loyalty oath of sorts, like ones we recited when we joined the Boy Scouts or Girl Scouts. For Christians, the classic belief statement is found in the Apostle's creed: "I believe in one God, maker of heaven and earth. . . ." For Jews, the Shema, "Hear, O Israel: The Lord our God is one Lord," is a statement of belief. For Muslims "There is no god but Allah, and Muhammed is the messenger of God" is a founding belief.

On a very general level, *believing* is taken to mean, "Yes, I agree with that." When I affirm such a statement of belief, I can then identify myself with a particular religion or organization. But sadly, many of us treat statements of religious belief on the same level as we do our everyday beliefs, say in gravity. In other words, we take them for granted. We treat such statements as factual, rather than as more integral to how we live our lives.

In contrast to this rather everyday context of believing, there is a deeper level, as when, for example, someone says they believe in civil rights. Hopefully, that kind of statement means more than, "I think civil rights is a good idea." This deeper context of believing has more to do with how we live than what we say. It is one thing to say we believe in a Transcendent that is caring and compassionate. It is quite another to live our lives trusting in that Higher Power for guidance. In this deeper context, believing is not so much about objectivity and rational assent as it is about subjective trust and personal commitment.

If we truly believe in a caring and compassionate Ultimate Reality, our lives should reflect that belief in significant ways. As was suggested earlier, we may need to reassess those early childhood images and metaphors we associated with God and let go of those images that were more fear-based than loving. It may also help to explore new images from other spiritual traditions that can broaden our entrenched personal perspectives. At the same time, we do not need to construct a grand new theology or philosophy of God.

Because we live in a rationally oriented culture, we naturally focus on our left brain's way of understanding and think we have to have something logically and rationally worked out so we can explain or justify our belief to others. But spiritual belief involves both the head and the heart. And the limits to reason are clear. We can never prove empirically the existence of a god or transcendent force. But just because we cannot *prove* the existence of this Force does not mean It does not exist. Just because I can't provide you with objective evidence, does not mean I cannot live my life trusting in transcendent goodness. And it is one's heart that provides the grounding for such a trust.

Without the heart's personal experience of the Divine, our belief remains hollow. At the same time, the heart needs the common sense and wisdom of the head, lest our emotions run amuck. So head and heart need each other's cooperation to better grasp the Truth. That said, given our culture's predominant bias toward rational, objective, head judgments, we would be wise to begin paying a little more attention to the sensitivities and leanings of the heart. As the renowned psychologist Williams James argued, "If your heart does not want a world of moral reality, your head will assuredly never make you believe it."[58] In other words, if your heart does not want to believe in a benevolent Ultimate Reality, reason and logic will never convince you of Its existence.

We can study all the great religious and spiritual texts and sit for years at the feet of a guru or spiritual teacher; we may recite dogmatic creeds, and give them our intellectual assent; but if what our head thinks does not touch our heart, we do not, in a deeper sense, believe. If we need to "figure out" our Higher Power before we can begin to believe or trust, we will probably never take that step. Still, it seems intrinsic to human nature to want to figure out Ultimate Reality, to wrap it up in a neat, easily understood little package. In fact, figuring things out may just be another example of our need to control.

It is not essential, necessary, or even possible, to figure out the Transcendent. There is, and will always be a mysterious and paradoxical aspect to our Higher Power. Instead of trying to figure things out, we need to trust and to surrender some of our stubborn self-will that insists on knowing everything for certain. Once again. other spiritual traditions can be a source of important insights.

It's a powerful double bind. Life is uncertain, and we want to trust and believe in a benevolent Transcendent we can never fully understand. And all the while our own ideas about Ultimate Reality are changing. That does not necessarily mean God is changing, but rather that we are changing. We just can't ever be certain we understand the essential nature of the Divine. I love this poem from Tukaram, the seenteenth-century saint and mystic from India, on the liabilities of *certainty*.

> Certainty undermines one's powers, and turns happiness into a
> long shot. Certainty confines.
> Dears, there is nothing in your life that will not change—
> especially all your ideas of God.[59]

If we can let go of our sometimes fierce need for certainty and security, we can, with courage and trust, begin to let Ultimate Reality come into and illuminate our lives. A friend of mine in Al-Anon likened this to being in a dark room and opening a door just a crack. If we just open the door a tiny bit, an amazing amount of light floods into a dark room. That's all our Higher Power needs, she said. Go ahead, brace yourself, and hold onto the door handle with all your might, but at least be willing to open the door just a little in order to experience what's on the other side. Let go of your need for certainty and take the risk. Be willing to explore something mysterious you may never fully understand. It is our ego, our own willfulness, that insists on certainty. But certainty comes with a cost—rigidity. Though we may initially feel uncomfortable relaxing our willfulness, there is also a sense of freedom and flexibility in not having everything nailed down rigidly.

### Faith and the limits of reason

Many discussions of faith and reason portray them as in opposition to each other; either you know rationally, objectively, and for certain, or you make an irrational, emotional, uncertain leap of faith. Too often what philosophers call "the leap of faith" is portrayed as abandoning one's sense of reason and sacrificing our brains to our feelings. But faith is not about believing the unbelievable and suspending our sense of reason. Reason and faith are not essentially opposed to each other. This separation is but another example of our culture's insistence on dualistic, either/or, thinking.

Thomas Merton, one of the most respected teachers and writers of spirituality of the twentieth century, knew from his study of the sciences that there could never be empirical proof for the existence of God. He also knew, from years as a Cistercian monk, that one could study and pray a lifetime without ever truly coming to believe in a Higher Power. Merton was far too wise to discount reason. He relied on reason and argument for most of his teaching. And he was brilliant. But he also understood the limits and pretenses of reason, and knew that if one's heart was not involved, rational belief alone was dry and lifeless.

In *Varieties of Religious Experience*, William James clarified the limits of reason and logic in religious matters. James claimed that the key to an awareness of the Transcendent is grounded in feeling and experience. Without the *felt experience* of the Transcendent, all talk of religion and spirituality is so much hot air. However, once one has had an experience of the Divine, then reason can use words to rationally explain it. But the true ground for our rational explanation is always the felt experience.[60]

Now it seems fair to assume everyone of us has at some level experienced an awareness of transcendent reality. As students in my spirituality class taught me, such experiences need not be grand or mysterious.

If indeed there is a benevolent and compassionate Higher Power that "wants good for us" then, despite our varied cultural traditions and life experiences, we can rest assured that every day we are being gifted with some of that goodness. A benevolent and loving God would not arbitrarily withhold Her love and mercy from some individuals and gift others. The Transcendent surrounds us. As Black Elk reminds us, the Great Spirit is "within all things."[61] We are, in Buber's words, continually being "addressed" by the transcendent Thou, but we may not be paying attention. Most of us are simply too preoccupied with, and distracted by, our busy-busy everyday lives. And, in that process, we miss what a friend calls these "god moments." What we need to do, is to slow down, entertain silence and solitude, and pay attention. Finally, we need to be open and willing to give up our preconceptions of how and when the Divine may appear to us. Ultimate Reality is full of surprises.

I have come to believe the deepest truths are always mysterious and paradoxical in nature. The problem is that many of us are uncomfortable with not knowing *for certain*. Even after four years of college and three years of seminary, I was still basically a dualistic thinker who wanted to see the world simplistically in either/or terms. I wanted the Truth be to a clear case of black and white, right and wrong, good guys and bad guys. I looked for confirmation of my either/or view in other religions and philosophies, but everywhere I turned the great spiritual traditions told me that Truth is paradoxical in nature. That's the bad news for us dualistic thinkers. We want certainty and we are confronted by uncertainty. We want a rationally defendable God, and we get a paradoxical Transcendent. The good news is we can learn to live with paradox and uncertainty.

## Doubt

Doubt is a word that is too often used in opposition to belief and faith. Doubt allows for a degree of uncertainty, which keeps us humble and saves us from spiritual pride. To doubt means to have questions or concerns regarding things with which we are grappling. And we are always grappling, in one way or another, with the nature of Ultimate Reality. Thomas Merton spent years teaching novices at the Abbey of our Lady of Gethsemani, reminding his students, "You cannot be a person of faith unless you know how to doubt."[62]

Given that the Transcendent is multi-faceted, each spiritually minded individual sees different facets of the Divine. No one sees them all. There will always be facets we miss; therefore, there will always be questions, doubt, and mystery. Belief and faith do not put doubt to rest, but they enable us to honor our doubts and, through doubting, to grow in belief and faith. Again, in the words of Merton, even when one has faith, "the unknown remains the unknown. It is still a mystery, for it cannot cease to be one."[63] The function of faith is not to explain away mystery, but rather to knit the unknown and the known together so we are more comfortable with reason's limitations and can rest from trying to figure everything out.

Honest doubt is a hallmark of faith and believing. It sharpens our sensitivity to, and awareness of, our Higher Power and helps us surrender our ego's stubborn need for certainty. Spiritual belief and faith are not unreasonable so long as they incorporate reason and remain flexible. Billions of rational, well-educated, individuals believe in the existence of a benevolent Transcendent. And reason helps them sort out the wheat from the chaff in discussions of Ultimate Reality. At the same time, all the great spiritual traditions remind us of the limits of reason, and assure us doubt is inevitable, given the mysterious nature of the Transcendent.

I believe, help my unbelief—Christianity

My ways are not your ways—Judaism

When you finally see through the veils you will say
This is certainly not like we thought it was—Sufism

O Wakan-Tanka, Great Incomprehensibility, hear me—Lakota

## Believing and knowing

Carl Gustav Jung, along with Sigmund Freud, is acknowledged as one of the seminal figures in modern psychological analysis. He and Freud made very different assumptions regarding human nature and took different approaches to analysis. But today we lump psychology with the other "hard sciences" and often assume they all have a totally rational and scientific foundation. Jung, however, is impossible to characterize in any such neat pigeon-hole as rational science. In October of 1959 John Freeman interviewed Jung for the British Broadcasting Company's (BBC) series *Face to Face*. That interview—still well worth watching—gives us a sense of Jung's wisdom and insights to human nature.

One of the first questions Freeman asked Jung, after inquiring into his early religious training and his childhood belief in God, was, "Do you now believe in God?" Jung paused, "Now? Difficult to answer." He paused again and a smile crept over his face, "I know. I don't need to believe, I know."[64]

Merriam-Webster's *Collegiate Dictionary* offers a long list of definitions for the verb *know*. One definition given is an archaic form, often used in Jewish scriptures. In that context, to know implied a deep intimate knowledge associated with sexual intercourse. To know someone, meant to have intimate knowledge of them—more than cursory knowledge or factual information. This form of knowing goes beyond mere cognitive left-brain affirmation. It assumes a deep experiential base. As you listen to Freeman's interview, you have the sense that this is the context in which Jung is speaking. He is contrasting belief in our normal parlance with his deep personal knowledge and experience of God.

Jung's response, "I don't need to believe, I know," again highlights the centrality of learning to trust one's personal experiences. It mirrors the insight of Reinhold Niebuhr, who felt that coming to believe in the reality of God can only be validated by one's inner experience.[65] It is only through deep personal experience—whatever form that takes, whatever the medium—that faith, belief, doubt, and knowledge come alive and help us make sense of our spiritual journey.

So, as we journey forward, let's take time to slow down and pay attention so we don't miss the "god moments" that surround us. As we begin to trust in our own experience of the Divine we will come to *know* our Higher Power in a more intimate way than we have before. Pausing each day for some quiet time and making ourselves available through solitude and prayer can be of great benefit in this regard.

**Exercise #5 Take some time before you write. Think of some old religious belief statements from your childhood . . .**

Apostle's Creed, the Shema, and so on. How would you write your own personal statement of what you presently believe regarding the Transcendent? Try not to be too wordy.

# Chapter 6

# On Prayer

*Now I lay me down to sleep.*
*I pray the Lord my soul to keep.*
*If I should die before I wake,*
*I pray the Lord my soul to take.*

Child's Prayer

This, my first remembrance of prayer, took place when I was five or six years old. I can still recall some of the comfort prayer engendered, though I'm no longer sure it's a good idea to have children think about dying before they go to sleep at night. Since then many of my ideas about prayer have changed, are still changing, and no doubt will continue to do so. I've learned much from friends, counselors, spiritual mentors, and a variety of wisdom traditions. And still have a lot of learning to do.

When I was thirteen years old, my father decided I was old enough to travel with him and his buddies on their annual fishing trip to Canada. Then, two weeks before leaving, another man imposed himself into the trip, and there was no room for me. Dad promised that if anyone could not make it, I would get to go. For two weeks prior to that trip I prayed, as fervently as a thirteen-year-old could, for one of my father's friends to have a minor mishap or disruption so I could take a trip I had always dreamed about. In retrospect, it was a rather wrongheaded prayer. But given where my head was, and my concept of God at age thirteen, it made sense. God was the Primary Cause of everything, a master manipulator. And perhaps some sincere and heavy-duty prayer on my part could influence the Almighty on my behalf. I guess the Transcendent chose not to grant my rather self-centered prayer, as I never made it to Canada that year.

That was one of my earliest experiences of "unanswered prayer" (or maybe the answer was "No!"). I had yet to learn that any prayer to a Higher Power is not a command performance, and that, thankfully, the Transcendent filters out wrong-headed prayers. What a mess the world would be if the Divine delivered on all the contradictory and confused prayers we humans offer each day. Two individuals each pray for opposing teams to win a football game. What is Ultimate Reality to do? Does It even care?

As our concept of the Transcendent grows beyond simple childhood images and metaphors, so will the ways in which we pray. But why pray in the first place? If we believe in a benevolent God, and yet accept that bad things occur without that God's direction or intention—for example, a tsunami tidal wave—just what does the Transcendent do? If the Divine does not act to prevent bad things from happening, how, when, and where does It act? If Ultimate Reality is benevolent and merciful, how exactly does this Force deliver on that benevolence and compassion? And what role does prayer play in communicating with our Higher Power? If the Divine is all-knowing, She already knows what we need. Why do we need to ask? Many questions surround the topic of prayer. In what follows we will focus on just a few key ideas and how they relate to our concept of the Transcendent; for how we image or envision Ultimate Reality determines to a large extent how, when, and for what we pray.

### The nature of prayer

Prayers for help, prayers for consolation, intercessory prayer, prayers of confession, prayers for discernment, centering prayer, prayers of gratitude, contemplative prayer. Prayer takes so many different forms; just what is it all about? The elders from the various spiritual traditions that met at Snowmass, Colorado, defined prayer broadly as "communion with Ultimate Reality." But they also added, "As long as the human condition is experienced as separate from Ultimate Reality, it is subject to ignorance and illusion, weakness and suffering."[66] One of prayer's primary functions, then, is to help us realize our connection with Ultimate Reality, so that we can live lives relatively free of ignorance, illusion, and suffering.

Prayer is also a means by which we establish and deepen our relationship with the Transcendent. Not surprisingly, the prayers we offer say much about how we envision the Transcendent. Since most Americans grew up with an image of God as all-powerful and the Primary Cause of everything that happens, it is natural that our prayers initially focus on asking for things, or to be bailed out of trouble, or for a Higher Power to influence situations in the ways we want them to turn out. If our image of God is of a stern Father, and we believe that we are born with original sin, then a lot of our prayers might focus on seeking forgiveness for our wrongs. If we envision the Transcendent, as did Rumi—all benevolence, compassion, and unity—then when we do feel loneliness, anxiety, and despair, we can pray for remembrance of the unity that already exists and for a dispelling of our illusory (though they feel real) feelings. If we resonate with Sallie McFague's metaphor of the universe as God's body, we might pray for the humility and wisdom to recognize our inter-relatedness and interdependence with the forces of nature. And, if our image of Ultimate Reality is that of a generalized Force for goodness that operates in the universe (a la *Star Wars*), our prayer might be less verbal and focus more on staying attuned to that universal goodness.

As our concept of Ultimate Reality changes and expands, it is natural that our relationship to the Transcendent will also change. As we age, and begin to experience more of life's inevitable disappointments, we come to realize we are not so much in control of our lives as we originally suspected. Through a natural process of aging, and hopefully maturation, we have more opportunities to experience life's uncertainties. If we believe in the existence of a benevolent and caring transcendent Force, it seems natural to seek Its help in dealing with those uncertainties. But how do we go about accessing that benevolence and love, and what can we realistically expect prayer to do for us? It is an exciting, fascinating, and lifelong journey. And we each begin at different starting points.

In March of 1981, after thirty-eight years of trying to justify my existence through work, pleasing others, teaching challenging adults at a nontraditional university, writing books, being too enmeshed in the life of my wife and her family, working as general handyman around our house, and rather compulsively trying to organize every aspect of my life, something finally snapped. I had obsessive thoughts of committing suicide, killing my wife, running over pedestrians in my car, and being stuck in elevators. The list went on and on. After three weeks of living in a downward spiral and a delusional hell, I agreed to my wife's admitting me to the mental ward of a nearby hospital. The life I had so meticulously constructed had simply fallen apart. I was suicidal, paranoid, and exhausted. I remember waking up in the locked mental ward and looking into the eyes of a wise and kindly psychiatrist who had helped admit me to the hospital. My first words to him were, "How could God do this to me?" He smiled warmly and said, "I think your concept of God is a little small."

He was right. My view of the Transcendent was pretty much the one I had grown up with—an old bearded guy in a white robe, sitting on a throne in the clouds, rewarding the good and punishing the bad. I assumed this God was somehow behind my nervous breakdown and was trying to teach me something . . . about which I was clueless at the time. It wasn't until I began work with a very wise therapist that I realized just how small my concept of the Great Mystery was. My therapist was deeply spiritual, but she relied on standard family therapy and seldom if ever mentioned a Higher Power. She also knew what I was wrestling with, and sometimes gently, sometimes not so gently, she began to open my eyes to the truth of my life. Therapy was not fun. In fact, the first year I hated it. But slowly it began to dawn on me how out of control my life was, and that there were actually some individuals smarter and wiser than me. Sometime, during the second year of therapy, my defenses were sufficiently worn down so I could begin to experiment with living a saner, more centered life. Therapy was still hard work, but it was good work.

Then one day, during a fourth year of counseling, my therapist looked at me compassionately and said, "I think I've done all I can for you. You know your issues and seem pretty much in touch with your feelings. You need to get on with the *spiritual journey*." Something in my gut recognized the truth of her comment, but my brain was not at all sure what it meant. And it felt like I was getting tossed out of class, a class I had come to rely on for both support and challenge. Although initially insecure, I did appreciate wrapping up one phase of therapy and was heartened by my therapist's dismissing me. But getting on with the spiritual journey? Pardon me, but what the hell did that mean? And how do I get started?

Thankfully, my therapist didn't leave me in the lurch and pointed me in the direction of a spiritual director who understood my situation. I met Jim Egan at the Cenacle, a religious retreat center not far from where I lived. Jim was a Jesuit priest: tall, good looking, and with deep-set compassionate eyes. He also had a great laugh. I immediately felt at home in his presence. I recall our first session and telling him what I thought I had learned four years after my nervous breakdown. He smiled and said, "That sounds like a break*through* to me." Then he said "Tell me what your relationship with God is like." I surprised myself by almost immediately blurting out, "I don't trust the son-of-a-bitch!" This in front of a Catholic priest. Jim just laughed. "Well," he said, "Anger is as good a starting point as any for a relationship." Thus began my spiritual journey.

It is redundant, but true, to say we all start from where we are, no matter how basic. One of my favorite lines from Elizabeth Gilbert's book *Eat, Pray, Love* is near the beginning when Ms. Gilbert's life has fallen completely apart at the seams—just like mine. She is in such pain that she curls up in a fetal ball in the middle of her living room floor, rocking back and forth. She has never prayed before, but reaches out desperately. She begins, "Hello, God. How are you? I'm Liz. It's nice to meet you . . . I'm sorry to bother you late at night . . . but I'm in serious trouble."[67] Elizabeth's cry for help was simple, not eloquent, and straight to the point. A friend from Alcoholics Anonymous once told me that the shortened version of the 12-Step prayer goes like this: "HELP!"

## Talking to God
> "Oh, Lord, won't you buy me a Mercedes Benz?"
>
> Janis Joplin

Prior to working with Jim Egan, my prayers consisted mostly of talking to, or at, the Transcendent, more specifically, asking for help. That may be the starting point for many of us. My image of God was pretty much that of a benevolent, yet stern, father/magician. Although not so crass as Janis Joplin's plea for a Mercedes Benz or a color TV, my prayers were for things I wanted, for altered situations, or to be bailed out of trouble, and, every so often, to find lost things. I learned those at my mother's knee.

When I was in the fourth grade, my mother lost her wedding ring on a summer vacation trip to Lake Erie. She was frantic and prayed to God to help her find her ring. After a couple of days she found it. To her dying day she was convinced God helped her find not only her lost wedding ring, but recipes, garden tools, phone numbers—you name it. Some older Catholics pray to St. Anthony of Padua, the patron saint of lost things and missing persons. Praying for specific things certainly is one level of prayer, but something I don't engage much in any more. Still, I do not demean it.

Given the mysteriousness of the Deity, who knows? If God didn't personally find Mom's ring, She certainly helped her search for it. And Mom's faith probably made that searching persistent and successful.

In any case, verbalizing our needs in prayer is important. Often we don't know what we need, or even what we think, until we put it into words. There is no magic here. Teachers and educators know that speaking and writing use different parts of the brain that aid in clarifying the thinking process. Journal writing clarifies my life experiences. And, when I sit down with dear friend for a heart-to-heart talk, I often don't know what is on my mind, or in my heart, until I speak it. The same is true of talking prayer. It clarifies. That's why talking to an all-knowing god is important. The Transcendent may well know what we need, *but It wants to know that we know.* And a big part of our knowing—or discerning—involves asking for our needs and, in that process, clarifying them. In so doing, we open our often-blocked communication channels and make ourselves available to our Higher Power's wisdom and compassion.

The Christian scriptures relate a number of incidents in which Jesus heals a person of a physical disease or mental illness. In many of those stories Jesus asks the person seeking healing what they want. Now, here is a sharp young Rabbi, who has probably seen this blind man at the city gate frequently, if not for years. And yet, when the man asks for help, Jesus asks, "What do you want me to do for you?"[68] Surely Jesus knew what the man wanted. There are many other stories in which Jesus asks someone with an obvious affliction what they desire. What these stories reinforce in me is the importance of our asking for our needs. Though I may only have glimpses of Ultimate Reality, I'm pretty sure the Transcendent is not co-dependent with us. That's why we need to admit we have needs and to ask for them even though our Higher Power knows them full well.

As a youth, and well into my thirties, my prayers consisted primarily of talking to God and asking Her to fix things or to bail me out of trouble. Talking—always me talking to, or at, the Transcendent. What kind of a relationship is that? Well, it's a little childish and narcissistic; but, like my anger, it was a starting point. Initially I had to learn to be clear what I was praying for. My spiritual director, Jim Egan, slowly and gently led me to see that prayer could involve, not only talking and asking, but listening and discerning. At first Jim had me focus on identifying and learning to ask for my nonmaterial needs—emotional needs like patience, courage, compassion, and understanding. Slowly, I began to realize prayer was also about clarifying where I was in life and what I truly needed, not what I thought I wanted.

Jim counseled me not to fret too much about the correctness of my prayers. "Just be honest. God will sort things out! And knows when what you are asking for is wrong-headed or stupid." That was really freeing. He also urged me not to hide my feelings. If you are angry with the Transcendent, yell at Him; He has big shoulders and can take it. At least your prayer is honest anger. If you are joyful, give thanks. Prior to my work with Jim, the only time my prayers were thankful were blessings at mealtime. And, to be honest, those prayers were more a matter of habit than of genuine gratitude. There is a saying in 12-Step groups that gratitude is one of the surest signs of a healthy recovery. It occurs when we stop feeling sorry for ourselves and acknowledge some good things exist in our life . . . things we can be thankful for. Meister Ekhart (1260-1328), one of the greatest mystics of all times, said that if the only prayer one ever offered in life was "Thank you," that would be sufficient.[69]

So talking to God *is* a meaningful form of prayer. The most difficult part is discerning why and for what we are praying. I'm always pretty sure I know what I want, but what I want and what I need are often two very different things. If I am concerned about the outcome of a particular situation, I need to let go of my ego and look at the bigger picture. Asking the Divine to influence a situation I have a vested interest in assumes I know best what the outcome should be, and I have to help influence Her toward the right (that is, my) outcome. And isn't that a little grandiose? So I need to learn to pray wisely and not assume I know what the best outcome is of any situation. More and more I have come to believe that prayer is not about asking for certain things or outcomes, but for emotional support and guidance from the Divine, whatever the outcome. Asking, and then being silent and listening.

## Consciously listening to God

But what are we listening for? That again depends on how we envision the Transcendent. If we grew up with an almighty, all-powerful kingly god, then might we not expect our prayer to be answered through powerful and dramatic signs? The Jewish scriptures, however, tell a different story of the prophet Elijah, who goes to a mountaintop to hear

God's word. There he experiences powerful forces of nature. The scriptures say, "but God was not in the wind . . . and God was not in the earthquake . . . and after the earthquake a fire, but God was not in the fire . . . and after the fire a still small voice"[70] For Elijah, God did not speak in a dramatic fashion but in a still small voice. And, if our Higher Power often does speak in a *still small voice*, then it is important we learn how to quiet ourselves and listen attentively.

Mary Oliver captures the essence of talking prayer, and listening for a response, simply and profoundly in her poem "Praying," which focuses on gratitude.

> It doesn't have to be
> the blue iris, it could be
> weeds in a vacant lot, or a few
> small stones; just
> pay attention, then patch
>
> a few words together and don't try
> to make them elaborate, this isn't
> a contest but the doorway
>
> into thanks, and *a silence in which*
> *another voice may speak.*[71]

The problem is that many of us are waiting for Ultimate Reality to speak to us as we expect to hear It and not as that Force may choose to speak. If we can let go old confining images of God, we can begin to be open to recognizing new ways the Transcendent may speak to us. If you don't recognize that other "voice" Mary Oliver refers to, keeping listening. It may take time to feel comfortable praying this way and listening for a response from your Higher Power. In my experience, it takes not only time but great patience and attentiveness.

There is a story many of you have heard before that illustrates how our expectations of prayer often create blind spots in our perception. There was a flood, and a woman climbed to the top of her house as the waters rushed by. She prayed for God to save her. Soon a motorboat came by and tried to assist her, but she replied, "No, I am waiting for God to save me." The waters got higher and a helicopter appeared overhead with a rescue basket, but the woman again waved it off. "No, I am waiting for God to save me." Finally, a large cow swam by and uncharacteristically spoke to the woman and asked her to climb on its back. The woman was shaken but once again refused. The waters got higher, and the woman was swept away and died. When she got to heaven's waiting room she was angry. She said to the gatekeeper, "I have a score to settle with God." The gatekeeper said God was expecting that and handed her a personal note from the Almighty. It said, "What's the problem? You prayed and I sent a rescue boat, a helicopter. Then I even sent a talking cow. What were you waiting for?" Perhaps we all need to be prepared for the unexpected when we ask the Divine to answer our prayer.

My spiritual director always ends each session by asking "What is your heart's deepest desire at this time?" That's an excellent question. What is your deepest desire at this moment? Pray for that . . . and don't worry. The Transcendent will sort things out. Try to be completely open and honest. Just as anger and thanksgiving are legitimate motivations for prayer, so are the despair, hopelessness, and doubt that, at some point, enter everyone's spiritual life. Simplicity is the key. I love the short prayer attributed to Reinhold Niebuhr's brother, H. Richard Niebuhr, on the occasion of one of his spiritual struggles. This from one of the most respected, brilliant, and reverent theologians of the twentieth century. It is simple, and honest and incorporates Richard's doubt.

*"God, if there is a God, save my soul, if I have a soul."*[72]

### Different modes of prayer

Recently I was talking with a friend who had made a decision to leave his church. When I asked if he missed church, Dick replied, "Oh, I miss some of the folks, but I don't really miss the services; they always seemed a little stuffy to me." I can be a little pushy at times, so I added, "Well, do you still believe in a Higher Power?" "Oh, definitely," Dick responded, "and I am taking time for longer walks in our nearby park and lying down after dinner and listening to classical music. I guess you could say that's how I pray now, by walking in nature and listening to music."

I can readily identify with quiet walks in nature and listening to music as ways of making contact with the Transcendent. Anything that breaks me out of the rush-rush of everyday living and provides a bit of solitude helps me in that regard. I would call these examples of *unconscious* contact with the Transcendent, and they are important touch-points with the Divine. More and more I experience these unconscious contacts with God when I am in nature. But I also believe the discipline of establishing *conscious contact* with the Transcendent is very important. In addition to talking to God, and simply being quiet, all spiritual traditions emphasize the discipline of some form of listening prayer.

As I mentioned earlier, when I first began to work with Jim Egan my prayer was all about talking to or at God. I am embarrassed to say that at the age of forty I had never remotely considered being quiet and listening for a response. Listening prayer takes a number of different forms. But all have in common the quieting or centering of our too-busy lives. I'll mention here just a few approaches. The bibliography at the close of this book offers more resources to consider.

Thomas Merton, the contemplative Christian monk, describes a process called *lectio divina*, which involves reading a short verse or selection from scripture and then just sitting quietly with it—not necessarily thinking about it so much as entering into it. Imagine yourself actually present in the text you are reading. Rest there and listen to your heart. How do you feel? What would you be doing? Bring that to your Higher Power. In my first few weeks working with Jim Egan, he assigned me the story of Jesus and his disciples in a boat crossing a raging sea. He asked me to get into the boat and to report back to him next week what that experience felt like and what I saw myself doing. At our next meeting my response was short; "I was terrified, and bailing like all hell." The practice of *lectio divina* helps us enter into readings on a powerful and personal level. I continued to work with that scripture for a number of months and learned a lot about my fears and how little trust I actually had in a benevolent Transcendent.

*Centering prayer*, another technique of quieting ourselves and listening, is often done in groups. Usually the leader of centering prayer begins with a short thematic reading to help focus the prayer. At the beginning of centering prayer it often helps to slow the breathing and to recite a short centering phrase or mantra over and over as a way of screening out exterior noises and interruptions. Silence is then entered into with the soft ringing of chimes or a "singing bowl." Silence may last as long as thirty or forty minutes. Then the leader again calls the group back to consciousness with the chimes or bowl. Sometimes individuals share their experience when the silence is ended, and the group often closes with a final prayer.

Centering prayer is usually done in small groups, sitting quietly in a circle, in comfortable, yet straight-backed, chairs. Almost all forms of listening prayer I know emphasize the importance of sitting up straight, though not rigid, with one's feet on the ground. Zen practitioners usually sit on a light cushion on the ground and assume a variety of back-erect postures. Don't tempt yourself by lying down to pray. Your body well knows what the prone position means and is so conditioned that it is difficult, if not impossible, to remain conscious. Centering prayer practitioners advise sitting upright and not slouching. Your body sends and receives certain messages of alertness when your spinal column is more, not less, erect. At the same time, don't sit in an unnaturally rigid pose. Relaxed, deep breathing is also an important part of centering prayer. Most traditions of spiritual practice encourage focusing on regular deep breathing (from the diaphragm) as a means of entering into prayer.

Prayer for *discernment* is another general type of listening prayer in which you turn a specific problem or decision or concern over to your Higher Power after verbally clarifying what that concern is about. Discerning prayer involves another layer of letting go and trusting that your Higher Power cares for you and can speak to your needs through your head, heart, and physical senses. The focus of discerning prayer is to become aware of God's will for us, that is, the good our Higher Power intends for us. In the next chapter we will take some time to reconsider our understandings of "God's will" and to let go of some of those unhelpful images from the past. So don't let that phrase hang you up right now. Actually all of prayer is about discerning the intention, or will, of the Great Mystery. The act of praying for discernment is a simple, yet powerful, way to acknowledge that we need clarification and help in how we lead our lives. It is a positive form of surrender in which we acknowledge our trust in a Force greater than ourselves.

**Preparation for prayer**

Most forms of both talking and listening prayer require silence and, at some point, solitude. Sadly, silence and solitude are difficult to find in our busy, everyone-connected culture. So long as our lives are busy, noisy, hurried, and otherwise full, it will be difficult to establish conscious contact with our Higher Power. As Thomas Keating offers, "Silence is God's first language; everything else is just a poor translation."[73] We need to take the risk of slowing down and being quiet. But we are so used to noise, we may need to practice withdrawing from some of that noise.

The monk Thomas Merton was well accustomed to the benefits of solitude and silence. In his book *The Silent Life*, he writes, "Not all (of us) are called to be hermits, but all need enough silence and solitude in their lives to enable the deep inner voice of their own true self to be heard at least occasionally."[74] Yet solitude and silence are not always experienced as something positive.

In the spirituality classes I taught at Metropolitan State University one of the first homework assignments was for each student to set aside one hour before our second class to simply be alone and quiet, without any interruptions. Longer and more explicit instructions were given, but the point of the exercise was for students to write a one-page report on how they experienced that hour of silence and solitude. In classes that typically numbered twenty adult students, I was always surprised how often the majority of the students found that exercise challenging and/or negative. They were so unaccustomed to solitude and quiet that, as one student aptly said, "It drove me bonkers!"

It seems clear many of us are so used to noise and distraction that, without them, we often find silence and solitude uncomfortable. The older I get, the more I realize one has to, at some point, make a conscious decision to withdraw from some of the noise and busyness of our culture. Our sanity demands it.

Silent prayer can begin as simply as taking five minutes each day to sit quietly and reflect on a reading. For years I jogged around a lake near my home, a run of close to three miles, at an easy pace. I did that religiously three times a week for many years. My warm-up, jogging, warm-down, and shower took an hour and a half for each workout—almost five hours a week. Yet, while I could discipline my body for those five hours, I could never take even *five minutes* each day to sit quietly. I tried, time and time again, but just couldn't do it. Perhaps part of my difficulty in setting aside some quiet time was my fear of solitude. As a master of busyness and codependency, I felt strange being alone and quiet.

Prayer is like any other discipline. You just keep at it. Today, for me, swimming three times a week has replaced jogging. I don't always feel like going to the YMCA for a swim, but I do it. Likewise, I don't always feel like praying each morning and sitting in silence, but I do it. Learning a new healthy habit is sometimes difficult, and I am slow learner. Just setting aside five minutes of quiet time each morning takes discipline. I chaffed at first, but quiet time is now a regular part of each day. And, like swimming, the discipline of prayer is a both a mental and a physical activity. Body, mind, and spirit are interrelated and interdependent. Just as your brain builds new neuron circuits to communicate with developing muscles when you learn to swim, so the discipline of regular prayer also builds new neuron circuits. *There is nothing magical about the discipline of prayer.* Learning to pray is like learning any other new habit; it takes time, patience, and repetition.

Try setting aside some regular quiet time each day, and find a place, away from work, family obligations, and your cell phone. If you are partnered, or live with others, let folks know that you are setting this time aside and ask them to honor it by not disturbing you. Look for a quiet atmosphere, and if that means leaving where you live and finding another sanctuary, do so—maybe a library or local coffee shop.

Then, as was mentioned before, find a comfortable chair to sit upright in, and initially focus on your breathing. Many individuals burn a small candle to help prepare them for prayer. Relax. Don't try to figure things out. Prayer is not a head trip. A short reading or poem may help you slow down and get centered. Stick with your daily discipline, even if you feel nothing is happening. Something probably is. Be patient, but be prepared for Ultimate Reality to speak to you on its own terms. And pay particular attention to your feelings, and other messages from the right (feeling) side of your brain; for it is at the emotional level that we most profoundly experience benevolence, mercy, and compassion.

### Prayer with and for Others—intercessory prayer, communal prayer, and ritual

Praying in silence and in solitude are important disciplines in any spiritual life, but so is praying communally and with others. Sometimes we need the presence and wisdom of another person to help us discern what is going on in our spiritual life. There are times when our most authentic prayer comes from the very depths of our being—prayers we cannot verbalize and do not even recognize. In the words of St. Paul,

... the Spirit helps us in our weakness; for we do not know how to pray as we ought, but the Spirit intercedes for us with sighs too deep for words.[75]

When my sister's daughter was shot to death, Barbara spent a lot of time grief counseling with her minister. She told me that, at one of those first sessions, she said to her minister, with tears flowing down her cheeks, "I can't even pray. I can't pray to God." Her minister responded, wisely and compassionately, "Your tears are your prayers." That comment was immensely helpful, and something my sister, in her deep grief, needed help recognizing.

I believe we all can use some help in developing our prayer life. But when you seek help, it is important to share your concerns with a close friend, mentor, or companion also on the spiritual journey. The practice of *spiritual direction* has become increasingly popular in the past two decades. Originally spiritual direction (or guidance, or mentoring), was a Catholic practice, based on the teachings of St. Ignatius of Loyola. Now a number of churches offer training programs. Individuals are trained not so much to "direct" as to accompany fellow seekers in reflecting on how the Transcendent impacts their daily lives. The spiritual mentors I most trust are those who have had formal training in Ignatian prayer and who take part in on-going supervision with fellow mentors.

*Intercessory prayer*, praying for others, takes a number of different forms. For many, it is a regular part of their daily prayer. In some Christian denominations, a little time is set aside after the sermon or homily for what is called "prayers of the people." It is a time when members of the congregation can stand up and ask for prayers for specific needs and/or healings. After the individual has spoken, the congregation may reply "God hear our prayer," or, even more affirmatively "God *hears* our prayer." I believe that there is great power in the many forms of communal prayer and that they function to create a common ground of concern as we open our prayerful hearts to others.

Silent communal prayer is another powerful experience. For six years my wife and I worshipped with a Quaker community in South Minneapolis. In a traditional Quaker service, *Friends*, as they call themselves, meet primarily in silence, usually for a traditional hour-long service. The silence is broken only when someone feels moved by the spirit

75

to share their thoughts. It took me a few years to become comfortable with long periods of silence, but it finally began to work its magic and is one reason I can now be comfortable during centering prayer. It takes time for most of us to be comfortable praying in silence for extended periods because it stands in such stark contrast to our culture. But entering into silence is a great blessing once one develops the habit.

Communal prayer comes in many forms and styles and is often expressed through some specific ritual practice. Rituals involve performing the same, often detailed, symbolic acts and internalizing the emotional response. Although sophisticated folks may initially think of rituals as primitive and scoff at them, our lives are full of rituals. Indeed, they constitute a fundamental part of being human. Baseball players are well known for their idiosyncratic ritual actions before they come to bat. Most of us unknowingly follow ritual behavior when we get up in the morning or when we face a particularly challenging situation. The repetition and familiarity of rituals confirms something innately human and comforting for us.

In *The Sacred Pipe*, the Lakota medicine man Black Elk details a number of rituals important to Lakota communal life. A central ritual is the offering of tobacco through smoking of the pipe. All present participate as a leader offers the pipe to the six primary directions—west-north-east-south, Father sky and Mother earth. The smoke is an offering to Wakan-Tanka, the Great Mystery. The words repeated after each offering of the pipe emphasize the communal nature of the Lakota rituals—"that my people might live."[76] Communal prayer and rituals aid in clarifying individual and community needs and reinforce group bonding. In the words of the Lakota, "Mitakuye Oyas'in" ("all my relations"), ritual acts remind us that we are all related, all interconnected, and all interdependent.

Another communal aspect of prayer central to Lakota and most Native American cultures is that prayer is always done within the context of the ancestors. I am not referring here to prayers for the dead. In traditional Lakota culture a very thin veil exists between the living and those who have passed on. Every filling of the pipe is an explicit invitation to the ancestors to join in the ritual. Indeed, without the ancestors, there would be no rituals, and there could be no prayer. Again, the "sophisticated" may smile at such an idea, but, if we believe that there is more to life than this earthly existence, and if we believe some spark of the eternal continues after death, then it seems not so strange to pray to, and with, those who have "crossed over to the other side."

### How prayer works and its inevitable distractions

I once asked my spiritual director, Helen, "So tell me, when I pray how does it work?" She smiled and said, "We don't know, and isn't that a good thing?" That gave me pause. It was a wise response. If we thought we knew how prayer worked, then we would probably try to manipulate it, and it would become simply another means of trying to control the Transcendent. How prayer works is up to God. It certainly works on, and for, those who do the praying by helping to clarify our own needs. The Danish philosopher Soren Kierkegaard put it most succinctly, "Prayer does not change God, it changes the one who offers it."[77] Prayer changes the attitude, and often, the mood of the person *praying*. I know that when I pray about someone I perceive as a "pain in the butt," my attitude toward them softens and I see more of their humanity.

Marcus Borg, a contemporary liberal—some would say, radical—theologian, was once asked if he prayed for others, given that most of his theology stresses God's non-direct intervention (that is, God does not swoop down and rescue a little girl from the path of a drunk driver). Borg responded,

> I (still) practice intercessory prayer . . . I pray for my family's health and safety, for friends, for somebody I know is suffering, and for the general suffering of the world. For me to refuse to do intercessory prayer because I (don't believe God will intervene) would be to claim too much . . . So I do intercessory prayer because it seems like a natural act of caring, and because refusing to do so, because I can't imagine (how it works) . . . would be an act of intellectual arrogance.[78]

Those are pretty much my own sentiments. As to how, why, where, and when the Divine responds to my prayer for others, I don't have a clue, and am convinced that in this lifetime I never will. And, it really isn't my business. I allocate that issue to the realm of spiritual mystery. I do know that prayer for others does feel natural and it changes me.

Regardless of whether or not my prayer changes God and Her intentions, I believe it can, and does, improve my relationship with the Transcendent. And I like to think it may gladden the heart of the Divine that we care enough to pray—to ask for help and to give thanks. I also imagine it saddens our Higher Power when we choose the wrong path and live without gratitude.

The life of the spirit is no different from any other part of our life. There are ups and downs, times when we feel exhilarated and full of energy, and days when all we feel is the taste of dry ashes in our mouth. I know of no spiritual traditions that promise prayer will always be an uplifting experience. In the long run I know there are incredible benefits. But in the short run, and the day-to-day practice of prayer, while peak moments do occur, more often we know the discipline of "just doing it."

Then again, deep valleys also occur. Indeed, everyone I know who is on the spiritual journey talks about times when their spiritual life seems to run dry. If we expect it to be otherwise, we will be disheartened when the dry times come. A short poem by the Sufi poet Hafiz captures those spiritual ups and downs wonderfully.

> When I first began to love God,
>     I thought I'd fallen into the ocean,
> but I was only standing on the shore.
>     Then I entered the water,
> and was thrown back on shore,
>     and then washed again into the ocean.
> God, why did I want this love?
>     And what is this back and forth?[79]

The discipline of prayer in our spiritual life is not a silver bullet, protecting us from all the bad things that can happen to us. There will also be dry times, and there will always be distractions. Many of us have an image of spiritually inclined individuals as calm, serene, and free from problems, worries, and anxiety. Do not be deceived. All great spiritual women and men face "down times" and distractions in their prayer. In *The Wisdom of the Desert*, Thomas Merton comments on some of the stories that came out of fourth- and fifth-century Egypt, when many Christian hermits withdrew into the desert to escape the insanity of the then-urban life of Rome, to retreat into prayer and meditation. Novices would seek the wisdom of elders is dealing with the challenges of desert solitude and silence. It was not an easy life. A regular concern was how often young hermits experienced distractions and an inability to focus in their daily prayer.

A brother came to Abbot Pastor and said: Many distracting thoughts come into my mind, and I am in danger because of them. Then the elder thrust him out into the open air and said: Open up the garments about your chest and catch the wind in them. But he replied: This I cannot do. So the elder said to him: If you cannot catch the wind, neither can you prevent distracting thoughts from coming into your head. Your job is to say No to them.[80]

Where do these distractions come from? Perhaps they grow out of the normal stress and strain of everyday life, or from unconscious needs, or from a nonbenevolent source. It really doesn't matter where or how they occur. The most bedeviling thing about distractions is that "our hopeless efforts to put a stop to this parade of images, generate(s) a nervous tension which only makes things a hundred times worse."[81] The harder we try to ignore distractions, the tighter grip they have on us. We give power to distractions when we try to wrestle with them. As a recovering compulsive-obsessive person, I know my demons love nothing better than when I wrestle with them alone. *They always win.* The secret is to simply let go. Acknowledge that you are distracted, let these distractions pass through your consciousness, and bid them a fond adieu. And don't be afraid to ask for help from your Higher Power. Henri Nouwen, another student of desert wisdom reminds us,

> Anyone who wants to fight his demons with his own tools is a fool. The wisdom of the desert is that confrontation with our own frightening nothingness forces us to surrender ourselves totally and unconditionally to God.[82]

I am not sure it matters what specific form our prayer time takes. We start where we need to start and our prayer will change as we grow. Most important is that we maintain the discipline of setting aside quiet time for prayer and that we eventually feel comfortable with that type of prayer. Don't be afraid to experiment. Foremost, find a quiet place. Then take a few deep, relaxing breaths, rest your busy brain, and, above all, pay attention. And don't expect your first efforts, especially of listening prayer, to be all that rewarding. Make a commitment to stay with a particular form or method for at least a couple of weeks. Seek help from a spiritual director or guide. And be willing to surrender, or let go of, your own willfulness and expectations of how, when, and where your Higher Power will respond to your prayer.

## Exercise #6 Talking prayer

Most of us learn to pray through some form of *talking prayer*. Try to recall what your earliest prayers were like. Write down one briefly. How does your prayer today differ in form, style, or attitude? Briefly describe how, *and where*, you pray today.

Chapter 7

# God's Will for Us

*[Our] vocation is not to simply be, but to work together*
*with God in the creation of our own life,*
*our own identity, our own destiny.*

Thomas Merton

The concept of God's will, and how we discern it, looms large on the spiritual journey. Not surprisingly, how we interpret that will hinges on how we envision the nature of the transcendent. We have been exploring new names and images as alternatives to the model of a stern, fatherly, Almighty that many of us grew up with. Yet, even as we consider new ways of thinking and feeling about a more compassionate Higher Power, we have acknowledged that we can never fully grasp the nature of Ultimate Reality. In one sense, we are all blind men and women trying to get our hands on a "Transcendent Elephant." And, if we are only beginning to comprehend the nature of the Elephant, what can we ever know about the Elephant's will? That's a real challenge!

Still, there are some things we can discern. What if our Higher Power is more compassionate and caring than strict and demanding? What if this benevolent Force truly loves and cares for us, and wants us to have an abundant life? If that is the case, then we need not fear Its will as always harsh and demanding. What follows reflects my own growing belief that the will of the Transcendent is good news, and not to be regarded with fear and trembling. It is filtered through my experiences as a teacher of adult students, and especially my exposure to Lakota, Jewish, and Sufi traditions that have so enriched my journey.

My earliest recollection of struggling with a sense of direction in my life came while I was a college student in the early 1960s. I started out as a chemical engineering student but at the end of my freshman year was disillusioned and, in all honesty, not that skilled in engineering. So I transferred to a liberal arts college full of questions and not at all sure where I was headed. Why had I ever wanted to be a chemical engineer? Would my parents be disappointed in me? What's life really all about? Is there a God? I began reading. And, as a true child of the turbulent 1960s, discovered I was not alone in my searching and questioning.

The groundwork had been laid in the 1940s and 1950s by the existentialist writers Albert Camus, Simone deBeauvoir, and Jean Paul Sartre. The years following the horrors of World War II were a time of questioning—questioning just about everything, especially the existence of God, in the face of persistent evil. Another writer from that era who grabbed my attention was Victor Frankel and his powerful book, *Man's Search for Meaning*. Frankel, a psychologist, told his story of surviving internment in a Nazi concentration camp during World War II. He detailed how he and others managed to live through the horrors of Auschwitz, while so many others gave up the will to live. Frankel's story is not so much one of heroism in the face of brutality (though that is evident), but of his growing awareness that those individuals who had a larger sense of purpose to their lives, something they felt they had to accomplish before dying, had the best odds of surviving. In the second half of his book Frankel outlined a new approach to therapy focusing on the importance of helping patients discover something that motivated them and gave their life purpose—a cause, a calling, a passion. So far as I can recall, Frankel never used the term *God's will*, yet he powerfully raised the question of life's meaning and direction for believers and nonbelievers alike.

Is there a meaning or direction to one's life? Our primary assumption thus far has been the existence of a benevolent transcendent Force that "wants good for us." So, doesn't that assumption answer the question of life's meaning? Well, yes, and no. It's one thing to acknowledge that because a benevolent transcendent Force exists, life has meaning. It is quite another to ask how that meaning impacts on you and me individually. How do we fit into that greater meaning? Is there a plan for each of our lives? Docs Ultimate Reality have a special role for each of us to play, or we merely bit players in a larger celestial drama? Does God's will imply some specific task, or is it of a more general nature?

My own understanding of God's will has changed dramatically over the years. I grew up in a fairly liberal Christian home and was not burdened with a lot of negative religious baggage. Still, my earliest images of "real" Christians were those of preachers and missionaries who traveled to obscure primitive lands to do heroic work with poor people and to "spread the word of God" through religion, education, and medicine. With these models in mind, I used to think that the Transcendent had a specific job for each of us to accomplish—sort of an assigned life vocation. I'm sure my mother, who was quite a social activist, greatly influenced my perceptions. Anyway, as a child, I was actually afraid to seek God's will for my life. I felt that if I let the Transcendent direct my life He might send me to Africa to work in a leper colony. Honest!

Whatever else God's will meant to me, if it was authentic, it was probably strict, demanding of great sacrifice, and not much fun. And it was rooted in that childhood image of a stern old man in white robes, sitting on a throne in the clouds, and calling all the shots. That image did more to inspire fear and uncertainty than it did to help me discover a pathway in life. Apparently Thomas Merton was familiar with that image, and the message behind it. In 1961 he wisely commented,

> Too often the conventional conception of God's will (is) a sphinx-like and arbitrary force bearing down on us with implacable hostility . . . These arbitrary "dictates" of a domineering and insensible Father are more often seeds of hatred than of love.[83]

Indeed, it is this conception of an arbitrary, sphinx-like force that still fuels the contemporary view of God as the primary cause of all things—good and *bad*. I had a lot of growing to do before I could move beyond my childhood image of an all-powerful, arbitrary, sky-god to a more benevolent and compassionate Higher Power. My early liberal religious training may have given me glimpses of the Trancendent's mercy, but I still had a long way to go.

### Lessons from the Lakota

As I slowly, but surely, came to realize that the Transcendent was not "out to get me" and send me to Africa, I had a lot of teachers along the way. My work with Fr. Jim Egan and my exposure to Native American culture were pivotal points in this development. I still don't know how to put this into words. It was much more a right-brain experience than a rational, left-brain journey. But, through my exposure to Native

American cultures, I began to experience a grace and openness, a freedom, and lack of judgment, that eventually led me to a much more compassionate Higher Power and a more gracious, positive, and affirming vision of God's will than I had known before.

The first sweat lodge ceremony I attended set the tone. I had been invited by spiritual leader Amos Owen, of the Dakota Sioux, to attend a sweat lodge (purification) ceremony at Prairie Island, about an hour's drive from my home in Minneapolis. Amos said to arrive sometime around sunset and to bring shorts to wear inside the sweat lodge. I showed up on time (White man's time), actually a little before sunset. The small sweat lodge was obvious, and much smaller than I imagined, but no one seemed to be around. Thinking I had come on the wrong day, I went to Amos's home and found him and his wife relaxed and finishing dinner. I was welcomed and told that tonight indeed there would be a sweat ceremony. When I asked when it would start, Amos was intentionally vague. "Well," he said, "first we need to start the fire to heat the rocks." "Good Lord! " I thought. "They haven't even started a fire yet; this could take hours." To make small talk as others arrived and preparations slo-o-o-owly began to take shape, I apologized to Amos's wife for being early and for not coming down last week, when I had originally planned to visit. She smiled softly and said, "Well, you are here now, and that's all that is important." Not a hint of judgment, just gracious acceptance.

In the hours that followed I was taught how to make tobacco ties as offerings to the Great Spirit, and was told just enough to know how the ceremony would proceed. I was a little more than anxious, having told my wife to expect me home around 11:00 p.m. or thereabouts. We *entered* the sweat lodge a little after 11:00 p.m., and, from that point on, regular time ceased to be. It is not appropriate to tell what actually went on during the ceremony, but what most impressed me was the sense of timelessness and the grace and spontaneity with which the ceremony took place.

I was so fearful of saying the wrong thing or making the wrong move, all the while being packed into the tiny lodge, shoulder to shoulder, and butt to butt, with sixteen other sweat-streaming bodies. I was reassured there was no need to fear, and to simply relax, concentrate on prayer, and surrender to the ceremony. Nothing I could do would mess things up. What relief! And, in retrospect, how egotistical of me to think that I was so important as to disturb a centuries-old ceremony. I lost all sense of time and floated through the purification ceremony. I do remember, as we left the sweat lodge and stood in the cold night air, that clouds of steam rose off our bodies as almost a visible representation of purification. I drove back home through a late spring snow flurry, arriving at 3:00 a.m.

The purification that came to me was a release from my compulsive time constraints, worries, and my own ego. That experience of a gracious and accepting Wakan-Tanka went straight to my heart, and my head let go of trying to figure it out and explain it to others. Despite the sacredness of the ceremony, it was surrounded by grace and freedom. In *The Sacred Pipe*, Black Elk mentions how sometimes little children will poke their heads inside the sweat lodge and ask for a blessing. He adds, "We do not chase them away, for we know that little children already have pure hearts."[84] It was that feeling of grace and acceptance—a right brain experience—that helped me begin to envision a less stern and demanding god, and to consider a benevolent Great Spirit whose *will* for me was to simply lead a good life—in Black Elk's words, "to follow the Red Road."

The contrast between the specificity of the Lakota rituals, which Black Elk details in his account (such as, the directions the pipe must pass, the number of salutations to the Great Spirit), and the lack of specifics regarding guidelines for human behavior, is ironic—specific, detailed, ritual acts surrounded by an aura of grace and acceptance. While clear directions inform all Lakota sacred rituals, how the people are to act in accordance with the *will* of the Great Spirit seems to be assumed with little need for codification. I attribute that to the organic sense of community and the implicit awareness of the Lakota's interrelatedness and interdependence with all of creation. Religion and ethics are so tightly fused with everyday life that no one even talks of religion and ethics. The rituals of the sacred pipe are designed to purify men and women so that they can continue to lead a good life. Wakan-Tanka's will is simply that his people live humbly and in proper communion and respect with each other and with all of nature. And, in Lakota culture ceremonies, there is much more concern regarding The Great Mystery's will for *His people than for the individual.*

## Jewish wisdom—The Psalms

In contrast to the organic and generally assumed way of behaving of the Lakota, the Jewish people were formed under very specific laws, with consequences for behavior. God's will is clearly spelled out in detail, first in the Ten Commandments, and later in the books of Leviticus and Deuteronomy. This detailed law was intended to free people from their own slavery, but it eventually became its own worst enemy. Some of the more educated Jews, and especially their leaders, began to follow "the letter of the law" and forgot its intended spirit. Whatever organic sense of community had developed in forty years of wandering in the wilderness wore thin as Israel conquered smaller countries, became more prosperous, and flirted with other nation's gods. Rigid ritual performance replaced the compassion and mercy that the law was intended to establish and preserve—so much so that the prophets began to cry out against religious ceremonies and laws that were empty of compassion.

The prophet Amos, speaking for Yahweh, rails against king Jeroboam II. "I hate, I despise your feasts, and I take no delight in your solemn assemblies." *English Standard Version* (2001). Another translation suggests "I hate all your show and pretense—the hypocrisy of your religious festivals and solemn assemblies." *New Living Translation* (2007).[85] So rituals can become stale, meaningless, and hypocritical.

The prophet's most compelling concern is that the widowed and the poor have been treated unjustly. The prophets remind Israel that God's will is not as complicated as following the letter of the law. It is about compassion, faithfulness, mercy, and humility. In the words of the prophet Micah,

> You have been told, O man, what is good, and what the Lord requires of you: Only to do the right and to love goodness, and to walk humbly with your God. Micah 6:8

Indeed, God's will for Israel differs little from Wakan-Tanka's desire that the Lakota people simply lead a good and humble life.

It was during my early recovery—from breakdown to breakthrough—that I began to discover some of the goodness and humility that Micah spoke of. I began to read the Jewish Psalms. My spiritual guide, Jim Egan, asked me to set aside five minutes each morning just to be quiet and at rest. My rather obsessive, busy-busy nature made that difficult. Somehow

I just could not sit still and be quiet without my brain kicking into wild and crazy thoughts. So Jim advised some quiet reading time with the Psalms. In the Jewish *Torah* there are 150 psalms, pretty much identical to the 150 psalms in the Christian *Bible*. Reading one psalm each morning, and reflecting on what it meant in my life, helped calm my frantic busyness and was the real beginning of my spiritual discipline.

It wasn't easy to read and sit still for five minutes, but many of the psalms were cries for help and implored God to rescue the psalmist and his people. And that was just what I needed to hear during the early days of my breakthrough—help from a Higher Power and rescue from my own ego. Other psalms are pretty violent and call on Yahweh to destroy, punish, and annihilate Israel's enemies. Given my rather disturbed mindset, I quickly set those aside and began focusing on psalms that spoke to my confused and broken condition—psalms of consolation and healing. I even began to memorize a few, so as to have them on hand when scripture was not.

A few psalms became mantras of a sort, and I breathed them in and out. Psalm 69, "Save me O God! For the waters have come up to my neck. I sink in deep mire." Psalm 23, "The Lord is my shepherd, I shall not want." Psalm 42, "As a deer longs for flowing streams, so longs my soul for thee, O God."[86] Somehow, even in obsessive moments, as I repeated these lines over and over again, they began to work their way into my heart. And, in the process, my spirit calmed and my view of God's *will* as stern, harsh, and demanding began to wane. The *Psalms* helped me to begin considering a more consoling and merciful image of a Higher Power. I also began to reconfigure God's will not only in personal terms for me but also, like the Lakota Great Spirit's will for the *people*. In both cases my sense of the Transcendent's will started to feel calming and reassuring, with no hint of working with lepers in Africa.

### Christianity's good news

In *New Seeds of Contemplation*, Thomas Merton speculates, "How am I to know the will of God?" His answer is reminiscent of the Jewish prophets, ". . . whatever is demanded by truth, by justice, by mercy, or by love must surely be taken to be willed by God."[87] But how do those general criteria apply to us as individuals?

In 1967, while in seminary, I spent a year on internship, affiliated with an ecumenical church in Washington, D.C., The Church of the Saviour. Its minister, Gordon Cosby, preached a sermon one Sunday that I have never forgotten. Each year members of this church had to, in addition to pursuing a program of Bible study and tithing ten percent of their gross income, join a mission group that worked in inner-city Washington. Mission groups worked with orphaned children, rehabilitated housing, ran reading and writing programs for the poor, helped take inner city kids camping and many other things, all as tangible expressions of the will of God. Mission groups met once a week to pray and engage in their work. Gordon's sermon that Sunday was addressed to new folks who were planning to become members of the Church of the Savior and joining a mission group for the first time. What was unique about Gordon's sermon was that he offered advice on how to *not choose* a mission group. (1) Don't join a group if you think they could really use your help. You will only be frustrated yourself and become a nuisance to other members. (2) Don't join a group because you feel a sense of "oughtness" or guilt. Joining a group from a sense of oughtness is a "red flag" for future resentment. (3) Don't join a group because its task seems heroic and worthy, but rather because it excites you personally. (4) Don't join a group because a friend of yours is a member; find a group whose task attracts you.

Gordon said that one's primary criterion for joining a mission group, as an expression of God's will, should be that feels like it's *good news*. Gordon then became even more explicit and told folks if they could not find a group doing something that really felt like good news, they should start a new group; and new groups were starting all the time.

God's will as *good news!* Why was that so surprising to me? Why shouldn't I use my natural gifts, interests, and passions as a means for discerning the Transcendent's will for me? At the time, that was a radically new way of thinking about the will of the Divine. Why did I have trouble letting go of that harsh old image of working with lepers in Africa, instead of doing something I enjoyed and was gifted at, like taking inner-city kids on canoe trips? Why did the Divine's will have to be heroic, demanding, and fear-driven? Thomas Merton advises his readers, "Unnatural, frantic, anxious work, work done under the pressure of greed or fear or any other inordinate passion cannot properly speaking be dedicated to God."[88] What can be rightfully dedicated to God are our natural gifts and talents.

Now, when I think of missionaries like Mother Teresa and their work with the dispossessed, I consider them in a very different light than I would have back in my college days. Although I still cannot conceive of this work as anything I feel gifted with or attracted to, I truly believe that, for Mother Teresa and her followers, their work with the sick and poor *is good news*. How could it be otherwise? If they did not find joy and fulfillment in this work, they surely would have worn out long ago. Even so, such work with the dispossessed and down-trodden seems so heroic. Does God's will always have to involve something heroic? Is it possible that more mundane and prosaic work might also be the will of the Transcendent? What about those of us with different gifts and passions? Are there ways our gifts for singing, gardening, sewing, organizing things, taking minutes at a meeting, and just being a good friend, can also express the will of the Transcendent?

And what about when our life circumstances change? Is it not possible that our gifts, interests, and passions might also change? What about if I am no longer in good health and living independently, but dependent on the care of those in a nursing home? If our abilities and interests change as we mature and age, then might it not be that a benevolent and merciful Transcendent's will for us changes to accommodate those new circumstances? At my old church, a group of half a dozen elderly women, who were incapacitated and no longer living independently, formed a group and met together once a week to pray for peace and healing and the world's needs—not very dramatic or heroic. Yet some dark days I am convinced the only thing holding our insane world together is the existence of similar small groups of dedicated women and men throughout the world, praying for peace and sanity.

Perhaps a central human task, at any life stage, is recognizing what one's gifts are and then using them to meet the needs of others. God's will might just be at the intersection of our individual gifts with the world's needs. And there certainly are enough needs to go around. Further, if we have free will, might this not be another case in which we are called to be co-creators with the Divine of our own identity? Using our gifts in service to others . . . but what are my gifts? What are your gifts? And why do our own gifts often remain so hidden from us?

### Rumi—gifts from woundedness

In special instances one's gifts are obvious from the start, almost inborn. Consider W.A. Mozart, J.S. Bach, and any number of child prodigies who were just naturally gifted in a particular way. If their skill brought joy to them, then I'd say that may be an indication of the Transcendent's will. But gifted prodigies are rare. And, ironically, for many of us, our gifts develop not from a fortunate inheritance of musical genes but derive from common everyday life and from some painful growing experiences that at first may not appear gift-like.

A few weeks after my nervous breakthrough in 1981, a friend whom I had not seen in a long time called. He had heard of my recent stay in the hospital's mental ward and simply said, "I've been there— counseling groups, therapy, medication, and electro-shock therapy. I've done it all. Any time you want to talk, give me a call." What huge sense of relief accompanied that call. I was not alone. My friend's previous experience with mental illness was a source of comfort to me and a real gift, given my vulnerable state of mind. It was also a gift of understanding that came from his woundedness.

After three decades of work in 12-step groups, I am constantly reminded that often our most precious gift is a sharing of our pain, loss, and woundedness with others. Who better to comfort a mother who lost a son through suicide than another mother, who, years before, lost her son to the same tragedy? After my niece's murder, my sister began to volunteer at a domestic violence shelter for young women. She had a depth of understanding and some very practical skills that were a real gift to the counseling center. It is no coincidence that many helping professions employ individuals whose sensitivity is grounded in their own healing from related wounds.

There is an interesting connection between woundedness and healing I only began to understand through Sufi readings and poetry. In his poem, "Childhood Friends," Jelaluddin Rumi speaks of this relationship between woundedness and healing as we advance on our spiritual path.

> Your defects are the ways that glory gets manifested.
> Whoever sees clearly what's diseased in himself
> begins to gallop on the way.[89]

"Your defects are the way that glory gets manifested." My defects! How is that possible? Shouldn't I be ashamed of my wounds and defects? Look at your own life and reconsider an experience that at the time seemed to be the end of the world—an addiction, a lost relationship, a physical disability, a life-threatening disease. Think of the wise individuals who helped you get through this dark time. Perhaps their sensitivity grew from the fact that they had been through the same ordeal you were experiencing. There is great consolation and healing to be found in the presence of someone who has walked the same path you are traveling. They become for us wounded healers and teachers. In a continuation of "Childhood Friends," Rumi urges us to find a teacher, or healer, who can clean our wounds, "chase away the flies," and put a clean bandage on us. And he urges us to pay attention to this cleansing.

> Don't turn your head. Keep looking at the bandaged place. That's where the light enters you. And don't believe for a moment that you're healing yourself.[90]

It is through our defects and woundedness that the light enter us. What a brilliant reversal of conventional wisdom. My wounds and defects (through healing) can help others. Alcoholics Anonymous first started when two "drunks" got together and began sharing their pain and their life failures with each other. They had learned from their experience. The principle applies to this day in so many recovery programs.

The first time I shared the story of my nervous breakthrough in Al-Anon, a woman came up to me after meeting on the brink of tears. "Thank you! Thank you!" she said. I was honored that she found my words so wise and inspiring, *but that was not the case*. What was most meaningful to her was simply that I had talked openly, and without shame, about my nervous breakdown experience. It was healing just for her to know she was not alone. In the process she began to lose what a therapist friend of mine calls her "terminal uniqueness"—the feeling that she was special and alone in her problems and suffering. Through sharing our woundedness and fears with each other, we can let go of this self-imposed isolation and rejoin the human family. For, in sharing our woundedness, we also share our experience, strength, and hope.

## Discovering our gifts and meeting the world's needs

Tis a gift to be simple, tis a gift to be free.
Tis a gift to come down where we ought to be.
And when we find ourselves in that place just right,
T'will will be in the valley of love and delight. *Old Quaker Hymn*

Where "ought" we to be? Where is "that place just right"? This old Quaker hymn impies that we find the "valley of love and delight" in part by being simple and free—not guilty and driven and enslaved. Our gifts can help take us there if we but recognize them.

Because of our life's history, its joys and sorrows, our accomplishments and our defeats, and often because of the shape of our individual wounds, we each develop different gifts. Not all our gifts derive from painful experiences. But, if our gifts are closely tied to our woundedness, and these gifts can be instruments of our Higher Power's love, then why not share them with others? Sometimes we are a little dense about what our gifts actually are. Want to know what your gifts are? Take a big risk and ask a colleague, friend, or lover. They will tell you. And you may be surprised.

It always amazes me how long it takes many of us to acknowledge our individual gifts. Too often the demons of self-deprecation and a sense of worthlessness make it almost impossible to hear the good news of our gifts. Our friends and colleagues are more likely to know our gifts than are we. It helps if we can begin to accept praise from others when they acknowledge our gifts. Do you have difficulty, as I do, accepting honest praise from others? It is important to let in the praise of others, for in so doing we are not puffing up ourselves, but acknowledging a gift from the Friend. And that is the key to accepting praise and not getting prideful. It helps to recognize that, however our gifts developed, the Transcendent was instrumental in forming them. Yes, they are our gifts, but we are children of Wakan-Tanka, and we do not own those gifts.

Once we recognize and can accept our individual gifts, we can quit complaining they are not the gifts we might have wanted. You may have wanted to be a great cook, when actually you are a better bottle-washer. You might want to be a charismatic leader, when your real gift is listening to others. You may want to be on the cutting edge of social justice issues, when your real gifts are with visiting the elderly in nursing homes. Accepting individual gifts is, I believe, a mark of maturity. It is also a wonderfully freeing experience. For so long as we envy the gifts of others and discount our own, we cannot "come down where we ought to be."

Finally, we need to take the risk of putting our gifts out there to be used somewhere. That might mean thinking of better ways to use them in our present job or life circumstance. Or it might mean making a move to a new job or even a new life circumstance. Above all, it means discerning our Higher Power's movements in our life. Ultimate Reality may not send us a personal e-mail. It may not happen overnight. But if we knock, somewhere a door will open and light will enter.

Let's close this chapter by revisiting that old transcendent Elephant. The fact that we can't know the exact shape and size of the Elephant does not mean we cannot know something of its general nature. And if we believe that Ultimate Reality "wants good for us," then learning to use our natural gifts might be an important clue to the Transcendent's will for us.

I no longer think that the will of Ultimate Reality means being assigned a specific task that we have no choice in. Perhaps, as Thomas Merton suggests, we simply need to work together with God in creating of our own identity and destiny.[91] And I believe that, whatever form it takes, it is the will of the Transcendent that we be healed from our particular woundedness—not made perfect, but healed; and that we share that with others. This connects nicely with our earlier discussion of human nature and how each of us is born incomplete without the presence of Ultimate Reality. Maybe the way each of us experiences Pascal's void in our soul is through our wounds. If so, then perhaps the Divine wants us to cooperate with Her and become co-creators of our unique destiny. In the process of healing and co-creating our identity—discovering our true self—we will recognize and acknowledge what forms our gifts take. But, in order to hear that good news, most of us need to slow down, pursue solitude, enter the silence, and keep an ear attentive to still small voices.

## Exercise #7

This exercise involves a little more risk than the others. Contact a very good friend and tell them that you are working on a personal project and need their help. You want to meet with them and have them tell you what they see are your gifts. Persevere till you find someone who knows you and who you trust. Then explain briefly what you are doing and why. Then just listen—Don't protest—listen. It might help to even take notes. Later, write down those gifts (character traits) and consider how you are using them in your daily life.

Consider another meeting with your friend to share what you learned.

# Chapter 8

# Busyness and the Challenge of Solitude

*A time is coming when people will go mad and when they
see someone who is not mad, they will rise up against
them saying "You are mad, you are not like us."*

Abba Anthony, fourth century

A time is coming when people will go mad . . ." Modern life is
stressful. As if we didn't have enough personal pressures, the result of job, family, and politics, we get bombarded every day
with mostly unsettling local and international news through television
and other media. We seem to experience increasing incidents of international terrorism abroad, while at home individuals go on murderous
shooting sprees. A dear friend often laments, "How will we know when
we have gone completely mad?" Perhaps we already have.

That is a rather sobering assessment in a book on spirituality, but
one that needs to be taken seriously. The bizarre and inconceivable have
become almost commonplace, and modern stress levels certainly play a
critical role in our human chaos. Life seems more dangerous and proceeds at breakneck speed. Consider the impact of today's sophisticated
communications systems, high-speed travel, and rapidly fluctuating international economics. In developed nations, all these potential sources
of stress give one pause to wonder whether our central nervous systems
are adequately equipped to deal with all that modern culture throws
our way. And in third-world-nations, poverty, hunger, and disease provide even more elemental sources of stress.

### Loneliness and solitude

How and why did we buy into this culture of madness? Spiritual
writer Henri Nouwen suggests the roots of our cultural stress and inces-

sant busyness are grounded in our essential loneliness. For Nouwen, loneliness is neither good nor bad; it is simply a universal fact of human nature. His insights mirror those of Pascal and Rumi regarding our basic inner void, incompleteness, and/or longing that can only be satisfied by a caring and compassionate Transcendent. "No friends or lover, no husband or wife, no community or commune will be able to put to rest our deepest cravings for unity and wholeness."[92]

But that assessment of the human condition need not be the final word. Nouwen maintains that our task, with the help of a Higher Power, is to convert our painful and fearful loneliness into a healthy, calming sense of solitude.[93]

Converting loneliness to solitude, though, is no easy task. First we must acknowledge our fundamental loneliness. Then we must face our human condition and honestly admit that, despite our sometimes fierce individualism, most of us do not really enjoy being alone. In fact, more often than not, we fear being alone. Again, Nouwen says it so well in his book *Reaching Out.*

> When we have no project to finish, no friend to visit, no book to read, no television to watch . . . and when we are left alone by ourselves we are brought so close to the revelation of our basic human aloneness and are so afraid of experiencing (it) that we will do anything to get busy again. . . .[94]

And our culture provides an amazing array of activities and diversions to help us get busy again. As a result, the very concept of solitude as a calm, often silent, sense of well-being remains foreign to us. We have become too accustomed to noise and busyness. And this is not new. Even in the 1700s, the Danish philosopher Sören Kierkegaard commented, ". . . in the world of the spirit, busyness, keeping up with others, hustling hither and yon, makes it almost impossible for an individual to form a heart, to become a responsible, alive self."[95] Yet we continue to pay lip-service to solitude and complain that we need more time alone and want to slow down. Then we get busy. Apparently solitude sounds much better in theory than it is in practice.

Years ago my wife and I lived next door to a large family with six children between the ages of three and sixteen. We were going on a short vacation and looking for someone to house-sit for us. I suggested we invite the sixteen-year-old girl to stay in our house for the three nights we would be gone. We thought she would probably love to get away from all the noise and bustle of her family and five siblings. So we checked with her parents, gave her the key to our house, and invited her to stay there while we were away.

When we returned, we thanked her and asked how it was to have the whole house to herself. Our assumption was that she would be ecstatic with the chance to get away from her hectic family. She paused, and then said sheepishly, "Well, it was really quiet in your house. I got scared and kept thinking I was hearing things move around. So I brought over the dog and two of my younger sisters. I hope that was okay." "Fine," said I, rather taken back. Only then did we realize how totally unfamiliar she was with silence and solitude. They did not comfort her; indeed they frightened her.

In modern culture we have become masters at avoiding solitude. Though I fly only two or three times a year, I find it next to impossible to find a place in any airport where CNN news is not blaring forth from a video monitor. Shopping malls, department stores, even auto repair waiting-rooms, all offer "music" of one sort or another to keep our minds preoccupied. Even when we are put on hold during a telephone call—"that is very important to us"—music and/or advertisements blare forth incessantly. We experience so many distractions it seems there is almost a conspiracy to prevent silence and solitude. So much so, that we need to reconsider the concept of solitude—what it is and what it is not—in order to get some bearings in our spiritual life.

> Solitude is not simply being alone. We can be incredibly busy and distracted while alone.
> Solitude is not merely rest. We all need periods of rest and sleep, but solitude requires attentiveness.
> Solitude is not necessarily silent. Consider the gently lapping of the ocean's surf or the soft flickering of a campfire.
> Solitude is not focusing on one's self and avoiding others, but serves as a foundation for community.

Henri Nouwen describes solitude as "a quiet inner center" and adds, "The movement from loneliness to solitude, however, is the beginning of the spiritual life."[96] The quiet inner center of solitude becomes the fulcrum, or pivot point, of our spiritual life; for it is through silence and solitude that we become open to that still small voice of our Higher Power. That's why the practice of solitude is an integral part of all the great spiritual traditions. But to achieve a healthy sense of solitude most of us have a lot of work to do—a different type of work than our normal busyness. And we have to be willing to set aside time from our busy lives to learn how to be unbusy.

I taught adult students at a nontraditional university for more than thirty years. In all those years my students' most common complaint was "I just don't have enough time." The vast majority of them had full-time jobs and supported a family. Some were single parents. Some even worked two jobs. I salute every student who, in addition to their regular lives, adds the task of finishing up a college degree. But their lack of time concerned me because I was also aware of it as a culture-wide phenomena. Most all of us complain we are too busy.

Though my students' complaints are very understandable, they are similar to the ones I hear from most of my friends—even retired friends. Too busy! Not enough time! But why would retired individuals have this complaint? One would think that having more time is why individuals choose to retire. Yet most of my retired friends are either full-time grandparents or busy "professional volunteers" working for worthy causes.

No one seems to have enough time. Enough time for what? We all have the same amount of time—twenty-four hours every day. And would our lives be any less busy if there were twenty-six or twenty-eight hours in a day? Could busyness and avoidance of solitude be just one more clever dodge from facing our human condition and need for the Transcendent in our lives?

### The culture of busyness

It seems every advance in technology promising less work and more freedom for leisure has the opposite effect. With more conveniences, we just seem to have found only different ways to stay busy and distracted. This is particularly true in the area of communication. Consider the impact of the Internet and so-called "social media" on our lives. They provide blogs, chat rooms, Facebook, Twitter, and Linked-in relationships that offer immediate and widespread "friendship." Just keeping up with one's daily e-mail messages can be a full-time job. I am not a very "Linked-in" kind of guy and have no Facebook account, yet recently, on return from a five-day vacation, eighty-three e-mail messages awaited me. In addition to the many personal communication gadgets, there are a plethora of Web sites that offer more opportunities to keep busy. Perhaps you have noticed how time seems to get lost when you are working on the computer.

It is easy to get lost in all the wonders of the Internet, and there are some wonderful opportunities available. However, the Internet also offers some less-than-wonderful resources where, in the privacy of our own home, we can engage in any number of virtual games and escapes from reality. One of the saddest forms of such escapism is exemplified by the popularity of pornographic Web sites. Pornography accounts for twelve percent or 4.2 million of the total number of Internet Web sites. Every second of every day over 28,000 individuals are viewing pornography, perhaps as a means of escaping their daily frustrations or their essential loneliness.[97]

Cell phones and their many ingenious apps (applications) are another example of how modern technology provides distraction in the name of better communication. Today I seldom see a young woman walking down the street without a cell phone pressed to her ear. The primary assumption underlying our social-media culture is that one should be ever accessible and available to others. Now, having cell phones for emergency use while traveling makes a lot of sense. And they work wonders in helping us find a friend at the airport. But something is seriously out of whack when we observe a young couple out for an evening stroll, and both are talking on separate phones to someone else. Or when we can't enjoy a meal at a restaurant because someone at the next table, dining with a friend, is talking animatedly on her cell phone—in a louder than normal voice—and ignoring both her meal and her companion.

Nineteenth-century writer and philosopher Henry David Thoreau made an observation apropos for today's incessant "communicators."

> When our life ceases to be inward and private, conversation degenerates into mere gossip . . . In proportion as our inward life fails, we go more constantly and desperately to the post office. You may depend on it, that poor fellow who walks away with the greatest number of letters, proud of his extensive correspondence, has not heard from himself this long while.[98]

But, sadly, most of us continue to be fascinated by social media possibilities, perhaps because of our fear of solitude and as a way to fill a loneliness that only our Higher Power can fill. An old Buddhist tale speaks powerfully of our relationship with a Higher Power and why we often fail to connect. A young aspiring monk visits his teacher for afternoon tea. The student sits down and the teacher begins to pour him a cup of tea. The teacher continues pouring as the teacup fills up and spills over on the floor. The student looks on in amazement. The teacher then turns to the student and says, "You are already full. I have nothing to offer you." He is not being cruel to his student. He is simply saying, "I can tell your life is already too full of others things. Come back when you have space and time in your life for what I have to offer."[99]

## Experiencing solitude

There are cultures where lack of time is not so problematical. I have experienced that different concept of time in encounters with Native American culture and, sometimes, in travel to foreign countries. In 1985, during a wonderfully laid-back trip to a small town in western Ireland, I got my first exposure to Irish time. One day my wife went to the grocery store to get some food supplies. It was a slow time of day, and there was only one person ahead of her in line. Only one person, but the grocer had to catch up on all the family news before waiting on Miriam. Ten minutes later he was ready to wait on her, and of course had to know all about where we were from. "Minnesota . . . oh my . . . and what are you doing in Ireland?" This took another ten minutes. In retrospect, what some might considered "wasted time" was really just another use of time and what the Irish consider everyday courtesy and conviviality. And it was surprisingly delightful.

Later on that same trip, three men came to the bed-and-breakfast where we were staying to connect a new telephone line. Everything was pretty much in place. All the workmen had to do was run some conduit through one wall and attach a wire to the telephone pole next to the house. It took them two hours. And of course they had to enjoy a "spot of tea" on the roof during a work break. After a week's time Miriam and I began to reset our internal clocks and to adapt to the time patterns and how normal life proceeded in Lisdoonvarna, County Clare, Ireland. It's hard to believe that not all people's lives are "run by the clock" the way ours are.

There actually are times and places when life is slower-paced and folks take time to converse with each other, and even to listen.

Of course we can withdraw from our culture of noise and busyness without traveling to a foreign land. I used to do a lot of canoe-camping in the Boundary Waters Canoe Area (BWCA) that borders Northern Minnesota and Canada. One trip in particular stands out in my mind. A friend of mine, a minister at a local church, was planning a wilderness trip for his youth group and wanted me to join him on a "shake-down" trip, as a sort of practice run, trying out his new equipment. Our second evening out, we had just finished doing dishes after a delectable dinner of Rice-a-Roni. It was a clear night and the dark of the moon. The stars were incredibly abundant, so we got into our canoe and silently pushed off a little way out into the lake. It didn't take long for us to realize that our trip coincided with the annual Perseid meteor shower. I don't know how long we rested back in our canoe and watched shooting stars race through the sky. But the light show was spectacular. Some flashed as bright as fireworks, while others seemed to trail endlessly through the sky. We spoke hardly a word and, after a timeless period of pure bliss, paddled back to camp and retired to our sleeping bags. Nothing needed to be said. It was, for me, a rare instance of experiencing solitude in the presence of another person.

So, if solitude is such a great thing, why do most of us avoid it? Why do we Twitter away our lives with social media? Why are we so afraid of being alone? Why are so many of us obsessed with being "in relationship"? Whether we are straight or gay, the icon of being a couple in relationship permeates our culture. Perhaps this craving for coupling is not so much a function of our libido as it is just another attempt to escape from the innate loneliness/emptiness that Nouwen, Rumi, Pascal, and other spiritual writers speak of. How can we possibly come together with another individual if what we are seeking is a fix to our own loneliness and emptiness? That kind of seeking becomes so desperate and clinging, and our expectations of the other so unrealistic, that the relationship is doomed from the outset.

Perhaps the strongest foundation for a relationship between two people is that each has a healthy sense of their own selfhood and solitude. The German poet Rainer Maria Rilke observed that "Love consists in this, that two solitudes protect and touch and greet each other."[100]

But interior solitude and personal integrity come with a cost. We are so familiar—though not always comfortable—with our false self that it takes some growing to shed this old skin. First, we need to acknowledge our innate loneliness. It is nothing to be ashamed of. It simply is. Then we need to look inward. The Buddhist writer Soygal Rinpoche says it well.

> Looking in(ward) will require of us great subtlety and great courage—nothing less than a complete shift in our attitude to life and to the mind. We are so addicted to looking outside ourselves that we have lost access to our inner being almost completely. We are terrified to look inward, because our culture has given us no idea of what we will find. We may even think that if we do we will be in danger of madness. This is one of the last and most resourceful ploys of ego to prevent us discovering our real nature.[101]

The monk Thomas Merton speaks eloquently of the benefits of solitude as an essential foundation for relationship and community. It is in solitude and through silence that we begin to discover the *true self* that is fully known only to God. And only when we are grounded in our true self can we authentically relate to and give ourselves to others. But we are so used to looking to others for our approval and sense of worth, we are so accustomed to the trappings of the *false self*, that only when we let drop all these external habits of beings do we have the opportunity to discover authentically who we are. The false self that Merton, Helminski, Nouwen, and other spiritual writers refer to is not in itself bad. It is simply our ego, that exterior self we present to the world—all our accomplishments, our job, positions in the community—who we are, and how we like to think we are when we have our best foot forward. In one sense a false self is inevitable and even necessary. The problem is that the false self assumes it is the whole show and becomes self-deceptive, for, in addition to our outward strengths, it also includes all our inward fears, insecurities, and compulsions.

The true self, on the other hand, reflects the spark of Divine that is in each of us. It is the self that has accepted its need for a Higher Power. It is what we refer to when talk about "really finding ourselves." And solitude is the place where we discover our authentic personhood. It is a self we can accept because the Transcendent has already accepted and loved it. Merton reminds us, "To be a person implies responsibility and freedom, and both of these imply a certain interior solitude, a sense of personal integrity, a sense of one's own reality."[102]

## An invitation to solitude

Our task then is learning to maintain a balance between the necessities of everyday existence and interaction and a healthy sense of solitude in the presence of the Transcendent. There are some very practical considerations. Perhaps the first task is to take time to find a place where we can slow down our racing engines and listen for that still small voice. One of the great windows through which I experience Ultimate Reality is nature. Paul Gruchow, in *The Necessity of Empty Places*, comments that getting to really know any natural place requires a solitude not unlike spiritual contemplation.

> If you would experience a landscape, you must go alone into it and sit down somewhere quietly and wait for it to come in its own good time to you. You must not wait ambitiously. You must not sing to pass the time, or make any kind of effort. The solitude is necessary, the silence is necessary, the wait is necessary, and it is necessary that you yourself be empty, that you might be filled.[103]

But we must make a decision. We must take the risk of experiencing solitude and seeing what it has to teach us. Here are a few tips I have found helpful in my own spiritual journey. Become aware how the media can permeate your life.

- Monitor the hours you spend watching television. Keep a post-it note on the television; keep track of the hours you spend each day of that week watching television; total them.
- Take notice of the types of shows that you watch on television. Pay particular attention to those you watch right before going to bed. What kind of a mindset do they leave you with?
- Monitor how much time you spend on e-mail each day. Again, put a large post-it note near your computer monitor to keep track. Then discipline yourself to checking your e-mail only two or three times a day.

Make a decision to intentionally pursue solitude by establishing some regular quiet time.

- Set aside half an hour each day for quiet time. You need not pray or meditate. Simply relax by going for a walk or listening to music. Try not to do anything.
- Turn off your cell phone during quiet times.
- Try setting aside one day of the week as your Sabbath, a entire day in which you keep your calendar clear of appointments and housework. If that sounds unreasonable, try half a day.
- Learn to say "No!" Look at your calendar and guard your quiet time. When conflicting opportunities arise, just say, "No thank you. I have something else scheduled."
- Try to do all of this with compassion and not self-righteously. You can withdraw from some of our cultural insanity without making yourself look special or judging others.
- Find a trained spiritual guide or mentor to accompany you on your journey.

Cultivate silence:

- Begin to listen for the sounds of silence. And take the risk of finding places where you can experience silence.
- The next time you feel lonely, try to stay with it, through the initial discomfort. Then, notice how you want to escape your loneliness.
- With the extra time now available (from not watching television) begin to explore reading some of the wealth of spiritual literature available. (*See* suggestions in the bibliography.)
- Begin keeping a personal journal recording thoughts on how your life is going. What's pleasing? What's disturbing? Special insights. You don't have to journal every day.

Learning to appreciate solitude is not unlike any other spiritual discipline. It takes time, persistence, and even (in today's world) courage. I love the common sense nature of Soygale Rinpoche's wisdom, reminding us that "spiritual truth is not something elaborate and esoteric, it is in fact profound common sense."[104] Developing our spiritual sensitivity does not mean sitting placidly on a large lotus leaf waiting for enlightenment. The spiritual and physical are not separate or opposed. Learning to appreciate a sense of solitude is like any other new practice—any healthy habit. It takes time, patience, and repetition for your heart to open up, and for your brain to build new neuron circuits. Seek out places where life seems not so hurried. As my spiritual director advises me, "Lean into the silence." Trust that you do not have to keep busy and that your Higher Power really will care for you. Accept the challenge. For it is only by taking the risk of solitude and experiencing some of its initial discomforts that we will reap its benefits, and deepen our relationship with the Friend.

**Exercise #8**

Choose just two of the suggested preceding tips and make a commitment to implement them.

## "Where Does the Time Go?"

The average American spends a little more than 24 hours per week, or roughly one-seventh of their life, watching television. Given an average life span of 84 years, and assuming you watch no television in your first two years, that translates to 11.71 years watching television. And that's not the scary part.

Presently commercial television runs 18 minutes of advertisements each hour, which work out roughly to 42 commercials per hour, and accounts for 30 percent of all television time. Thus, by age 84, the average American has spent 3.6 years (30 percent of 11.71 years) watching over 1, 289,433 commercials.[105]

### That's 1,289,433 commercials

Now, add to those 11.71 years watching television the amount of time one spends an average day on the Internet, Facebook, Twitter, LinkedIn and cell phone and that's where the time goes.

Want to add an extra 26 days to each remaining year of your life?

If you are presently an average American (and who would admit to that?) and you cut your television time in half, to 12 hours per week, you would have an extra 12 hours per week, or 26 additional days per year you that you would have otherwise spent watching television.

Chapter 9

# Continuing the Spiritual
# Journey

*Spiritual truth is always paradoxical.*

Parker Palmer

At the root of any spiritual journey lies the choice we make to believe in a benevolent Transcendent, Force, Spirit, Mystery, whatever we choose to call it. We do so realizing our choice is something we can never fully justify in terms of reason. It goes beyond reason and the ego's need for certainty. That decision to believe is rooted in our personal experience and feeling of the Transcendent's love and grace. Without such personal experience, spirituality remains pretty much a "head" discussion. Science, logic, reason, and all the tools of the left brain are good, and necessary, but they can only take us so far. And while we may never fully comprehend the mysteries of Ultimate Reality, we can experience the caring presence of that benevolent Transcendent in our relationships with others, and through nature, music, and a host of other heart-felt happenings.

The story of the blind men and the elephant reminds us we all "see" things differently, and in a limited way. It's not that our perceptual lenses are wrong. They are simply, and of necessity, limited. Our genetic inheritance, cultural rearing, economic status, racial identity, sexual orientation, and resulting life stories have shaped the many and varied ways we view life and inform our ideas and images of Ultimate Reality.

The good news is our perceptual lenses need not remain fixed. We may "see through a glass darkly," but we do see. And, if we are willing to take the time and effort, we can expand and clarify our range of vision. This is especially true in regard to our spiritual journeys. The spiritual traditions of Judaism, Christianity, Sufism, and Lakota cultures provide richly stained-glass windows deepening our understanding of both the simplicity and complexity of the Friend that Rumi says we all long to know. I hope they have been helpful to you.

We suggested that one important starting point on our spiritual journey is a willingness to reconsider some of the images, metaphors, and even feelings, related to the "god" from our childhood. My own ideas and feelings have changed rather dramatically from my early images of a stern Almighty father figure to, in teenage years, a more loving, less stern, male spirit. Then I flirted with atheism and naturalism, emerging from my college years believing in some amorphous universal force of goodness. On to four years at an inter-denominational seminary, where I encountered the feminine face of the Divine and Jesus' radical and paradoxical ethic of love. Post-seminary years introduced me to the wisdom of the Lakota. And Sallie McFague only supported the image of an interdependent and a more-or-less benevolent universe. Given my multitudinous shifts in perspective, it's comforting to hear again those wise words of Tukaram, from India, "Dears, there is nothing in your life that will not change—especially all your ideas of God."[106]

The most dramatic changes in my relationship to the Divine occurred during college and seminary years and my later "nervous breakthrough." Growing up as a white, middle-class male, privileged me to not suffer too many "slings and arrows of outrageous fortune" that Hamlet bemoans. Still, even privileged white males, at some point, become aware of their finiteness and experience bumps in life's road. And as those bumps—sometimes wrecks—inevitably came along, my images of, and relationship to, the Transcendent changed. As death, disease, mental illness, and family tragedies make their presence known, we are faced with choices between hope and despair and, perhaps most sadly, apathy. In the early years of my nervous breakdown, despair and apathy sometimes won out. I am not proud of those times, but they were part of my journey. Somehow, certainly not due to my own virtue, hope won out.

As we encounter the hard knocks life has in store for us, we all face choices, sometimes dramatic and sometimes subtle. Either way, no one escapes suffering. It takes a lot of courage to choose hope in the face of personal tragedies and harsh realities. For, as much as we would like it to be otherwise, developing and deepening one's spiritual life is no protection against the many tragedies that can happen to us and our loved ones. Mother Nature regularly reminds us that it not only rains on, but sometimes lightning strikes "both the just and the unjust."

## Facing the false self

Living with uncertainty and acknowledging that life is "chancy" is never easy—especially for those of us determined to solve the paradox of God's goodness and the inevitability of life's tragedies. As we begin to explore new images, metaphors, and ways of thinking about Ultimate Reality, we will need increasing humility to admit that our perceptions are limited and reason can only take us so far. And this means a willingness to grapple with, and accepted the limitations of, our false self.

Thomas Merton's wisdom in regard to the false/true self distinction has helped me live more comfortably with all the paradoxes the Transcendent presents us. From the outset it's important to understand that the false self is not bad. It is, however, limited. To view the false self in opposition to the true self is just another form of dualistic thinking that stands in the way of our relationship to Ultimate Reality. The false self is the exterior self, our ego. And, as any therapist or counselor will assure you, one of our first tasks in life is to begin to develop a healthy ego or source of identity—a more-or-less healthy false self—before we can let it go.

For a number of years Thomas Merton served as teacher and spiritual counselor to entering novice monks. He commented on how difficult it was for young men to comprehend the necessity of letting go of the ego when they did not yet have a healthy ego to work with. Most individuals who are now engaged in the spiritual journey often didn't begin until they were in their mid- to late thirties. We have to try making it on our own and, to some degree, succeed, before we can begin to realize that our ego/false self can be a stumbling block to spiritual wisdom. Thus one's first step is to develop an ego that recognizes itself as worthy. Beginning to experience one's worthiness and a healthy sense of identity is necessary before it makes any sense to accept to grapple with the limits of one's ego.

That's paradoxical, so let me repeat. We need to develop a relatively healthy ego, and recognize its limits, before our true self can begin to emerge. Don't rush the spiritual journey. Your true self will begin to make itself known as the spiritual journey progresses.

An old Buddhist tale speaks ironically of the difficulty many young adults have learning the limits of their own powers. A Buddhist teacher asks one of his students, "So, how are things going?" The student replies, "Fine." The teacher responds, "Good. I have absolutely nothing to offer you."[107] His tone is neither harsh, judging, nor cynical. It is simply reflects how things were for this student. For most of us, so long as life is running smoothly, seeking help from another source seldom enters the picture. Have you ever known anyone who said, "Well things are going really fine in my life. I think I'll start making some changes and begin working on my personal growth"? I haven't. As long as things are going "fine," why would you consider an alternative way of living? It's only when our best efforts to fix ourselves fail that we can begin to consider a new direction. That's why most do not consider a spiritual approach to life until they are old enough to some degree "made it," and then have fallen on their face, in one way or another—job loss, broken relationships, mental illness, addiction—or been brought low by a critical health issue. But first we must begin with our ego's illusion that it is sufficient to fix things itself.

Just as we have to, at some point, recognize the limits of reason and our left brain's efforts to "figure out" the Transcendent, so we have to painfully experience the limits of our own ego's power to heal our woundedness. The false self is like an old piece of woodwork covered with layers of lacquer and paint, hiding the beauty of the original wood (true self) beneath it. Just like restoring that old wooden furniture, discovering the true self requires a lot of hard work. It requires our attention and mindfulness and is best done by first simply slowing down our frantic life pace. The mind and ego are incessantly busy with projects, plans, ideas, opinions—thinking, planning, doing . . . thinking, planning, doing—always busy. Never still. When my godson William was a toddler and wanted to get my attention at adult-dominated family gatherings, he would get down on the floor, fix his eyes on me, point to the floor and yell "Uncle Chet—sit down!" Wisdom from a four-year old.

Each of us needs to learn to "sit down," be quiet, and listen. Slowing down and practicing solitude are not easy disciplines to acquire. And there is a cost to slowing down and beginning to let go of the false self. A good friend who, like me, is a workaholic and perfectionist, said, "I'd rather keep running. It seems whenever I really make an attempt to slow down, those demons who are chasing me start to catch up." Demons, obsessions, compulsions, character defects—whatever we call them—all form parts of our false self that we really would rather not acknowledge. But we must deal with our ego/false self, accept it, and never have the illusion that we can defeat it. We turn this struggle over to our Higher Power and trust that It will work with us to restore us to sanity and to recover the true self that too often lies hidden within. Even so, our false self never disappears completely. We will, though, become more aware of it and, as a result, it will not have as much power over us.

In order to do our share of the work with our Higher Power, we must scale back our busy agendas and take more time, in solitude, to reflect on our own lives, and to simply smell the roses. As was suggested earlier, it is difficult to hear the still small voice of our Higher Power midst all our noise and busyness. Buddhist author Sylvia Boorstein offers a wise antidote to busyness as she flips our cultural sensibilities upside down by saying, "Don't just do something. Sit there!"[108]

We might as well sit, for, rest assured, we will never be able to outrun or outwit our demons and defects. They are ancient and, in their own way, venerable. We must learn to live with them and to not be controlled by them. St. Ignatius of Loyola said, "If you don't tame your demons you will never know your angels."[109] We may not initially like our defects, but they are a natural part of our makeup and are keys to revealing the hidden true self. And, ironically, when we can acknowledge our demons/defects and accept that they are not going to go away, they also turn out to be our angels. How's that for a paradox? The fact that I suffer from perfectionism, grandiosity, and over-attention to detail can—and at one point actually did—drive me crazy. But those same defects, when tamed, also make me an excellent teacher of adult students—so long as I keep things in perspective. And I can learn to do that with the help of friends, recovery programs, and regular quiet time with that mysterious Transcendent. Being around others who are on the spiritual journey gives us the opportunity to learn from their experience, strength, and hope, and thus to become aware of the God moments that surround us every day. The choice is ours.

### Moving on with hope

When we do slow down, and start paying attention, we will begin to rest more easily with life's paradoxes and begin trusting that our heart has a wisdom at least equal to our head. In all my years of teaching some very talented adults, I can honestly say that the individuals who most often have difficulty making the choice to believe in transcendent goodness are the most brilliant. Intelligence, and the ego's insistence on certainty, must learn from the wisdom of the heart and our deep gut feelings that, all "bad things" to the contrary, there is somewhere, somehow, a force in the universe that "wants good for us," no matter how deeply we have been wounded. I believe God is constantly showering us with blessings even in the worst of times, and that the Friend wants us to work with Her in healing our woundedness.

Anne Frank was a fifteen-year-old child when she died in a German concentration camp during the Holocaust. For two years she and her Jewish family stayed hidden before finally being discovered by the Nazis. During that time Anne kept a diary in which she reflected on her life and times. Even with the threat of death ever-present, Anne Frank found comfort in those rare moments when she could experience silence, solitude, and the calm of nature. She wrote:

> The best remedy for those who are afraid, lonely, or unhappy is to go outside, somewhere where they can be quiet, alone with the heavens, nature, and God. Because only then does one feel that all is as it should be and that God wishes to see people happy, amidst the simple beauty of nature.[110]

Midst the horror of the holocaust, Anne Frank sensed there was a Higher Power that cared for her through the simple beauty of nature. She was aware of the presence of the Transcendent in the ordinariness of every day—though her life in a concentration camp was hardly ordinary. And that is the core of the spiritual journey: to see God in the ordinary of each day. To slow down our lives and to pay attention. To trust in goodness, even in the face of tragedy, and to look for that goodness every day.

# Footnotes

1 John Dominic Crossan, The Didier Seminars, Hope Presbyterian Church, St. Paul, February 27-29, 2004.

2 Daniel Ladinsky, *Love Poems from God*, Penguin Compass, New York, New York, 2002, p. 117.

3 Often quoted from various sources, originally found in Woody Allen's script for the movie *Sleeper*, 1973.

4 Chet Meyers, *Came to Believe: A Guide to the 2nd Step*, Gentle Path Press, Carefree, Arizona, 2010, p. 3.

5 *Joseph Campbell and The Power of Myth* conversation with Bill Moyers, Mystic Fire Audio tapes, Montauk, New York, 1999.

6 Miriam-Webster's *Collegiate Dictionary*, 10th Edition, Miriam-Webster Inc., Springfield, Massachusetts, 1999, p. 730.

7 Hebrew scriptures, 23rd Psalm.

8 Transcribed from audio tape *I Want Burning: The Ecstatic World of Rumi, Hafiiz, and Lalla*, Coleman Barks, Sounds True Recordings, Boulder, Colorado, 1992.

9 Coleman Barks, *The Essential Rumi*, Harper Collins Pub., San Francisco, California, 1995, pp. 168.

10 *The Sacred Pipe, Black Elk's Account of the Seven Rites of the Oglala Sioux*, Joseph Epes. Ed., Penguin Books, New York, 1971, p. xix.

11 Charles Brown, *Niebuhr and His Age*, Trinity International Press, Philadelphia, Pennsylvania, 1992, p. 46.

12 Sallie McFague, *The Body of God: An Ecological Theology*, Fortress Press, Minneapolis, Minnesota, 1993, p. 93.

13 *Sourcebook of the World's Religions*, 3rd edition, Joel Beversluis ed., New World Library, Novato, California, 2000, p. 1.

14 Jill Bolte Taylor, *My Stroke of Insight*, Viking Press, New York, 2008, p. 139.

15 McFague, p. 13.

16 *The Sacred Pipe*, p. xx.

17 Daniel Ladinsky, *The Gift: Poems by Hafiz*, Penguin Compass, New York, New York, 1999, p. 258.

18 Ladinsky, *The Gift*, p. 187.

19 Barks, *The Essential Rumi*, p. 27.

20 Martin Buber, *I and Thou*, Translated by Ronald Gregor Smith, Scribner Classic, New York, 1958, p.11.

21 Buber, p. 53.

22 RSV Christian Bible, Exodus 3:1-13.

23 Catherine Warrick, quote in personal conversation on topic of Sufism.

24 Barks, p. 261.

25 Paul Tillich, *The Shaking of the Foundations*, Charles Scribner's Sons, New York, New York, 1948, pp. 161-162.

26 Buber, p. 11.

27 Mary Oliver, *New and Selected Poems*, Beacon Press, Boston, Massachusetts, 1992, p. 110.

28 Yale University sermon, 1967. Personal memory from four years I spent at Yale Divinity School. William Sloane Coffin was at the time chaplain of Yale University.

29 *Joseph Campbell and The Power of Myth*, in conversation with Bill Moyers.

30 Buber, pp. 135-136.

31 RSV Christian Bible, Isaiah 55:7-9.

32 Blaise Pascal, *Pensées (Thoughts)* (Section Vii, 425) Many different editions.

33 Elie Wiesel, *Four Hasidic Masters*, Notre Dame, Indiana, 1978, p. 53.

34 *Sourcebook of the World's Religions* (excerpted).

35 Kabir Edmund Helminski, *Living Presence: A Sufi Way to Mindfulness and the Essential Self*. Jeremy Tarcher, Inc., 2002 p. 2. (excerpted from website source HYPERLINK http://sufism.org/books/livinex.html http://sufism.org/books/livinex.html)

36 Helminski, p. 3.

37 Ladinsky, *Love Poems*, p. 179.

38 Barks, p. 17.

39 Barks, p. 36.

40 Reinhold Niebuhr, *The Nature and Destiny of Man*, Vol. 1, Charles Scribner's Sons, New York, New York, 1941.

41 Niebuhr, p. 16 and p. 132.

42 McFague, p. 19.

43 McFague, pp. 74 ff.

44 McFague, p. 21.

45 McFague, quoting John Polkingham, p. 44.

46 McFague, p. 6.

47 Pope Speaks of Iraq and Tsunami in First TV Q&A, Rachel Donadio (reporter), *New York Times* newspaper, April 22, 2011.

48 Yale Divinity School magazine, *Reflection*, "Alex's Death" by William Sloane Coffin, November, 1983.

49 Niebuhr, p. 178 ff.

50 Niebuhr, p. 121.

51 *The Sacred Pipe*, p. 60.

52 "The Cornish or West Country Litany." Earliest record, F.T. Nettleinghame, *Polperro Proverbs and Others* (1926), but it certainly predates that printing.

53 Barks, p. 112.

54 Sirkar Van Stolk, *Memories of a Sufi Sage: Hazrat Inayat Khan*, East Wes Pub. The Hague, Belgium 1967, p. 27.

55 *Sufi Message of Hazrat Inayat Khan*, Vol. VIII, Motilal Banarsidass, New Delhi, India, 2005, p. 97.

56 *Sufi Message of HIK*, Vol. VIII, p. 100.

57 Albert Schweitzer, *Reverence for Life Sermons—1900-1919*, Irvington Pub., New York, New York, 1993.

58 *God: Readings in Philosophy*, Timothy Robinson Ed., Hackett Pub. Co. Indianapolis, Indiana, 1996, p. 138.

59 Ladinsky, *Love Poems from God*, p. 350.

60 *God*, pp. 128-129.

61 *The Sacred Pipe*, p. xx.

62 Thomas Merton, *New Seeds of Contemplation*, New Directions Paperback, New York, 1962, p. 105.

63 Merton, *New Seeds of Contemplation*, p. 136.

64 BBC Interview October 1959 John Freeman, *Face to Face*. HYPERLINK http://www.youtube.com/watch <www.youtube.com/watch?v=WQ8aV8YndwQ>

65 Brown, p. 46.

66 *Sourcebook of the World's Religions*.

67 Elizabeth Gilbert, *Eat, Pray, Love*, Penguin Books, London, 2006, pp. 15 f.

68 RSV Christian Bible, Mark 10:46-52.

69 Matthew Fox, *Meditations with Meister Eckhart*, Bear & Co., Santa Fe, New Mexico, 1983, p. 34.

70 RSV Christian Bible, I Kings 19:11-12.

71 Mary Oliver, *Thirst*, Beacon Press, Boston MA, 2006, p. 37.

72 H. Richard Niebuhr, prayer attributed to him by colleagues, during my four years at Yale Divinity School, 1964-68. New Haven, Connecticut.

73 Thomas Keating, *Invitation to Love: The Way of Christian Contemplation*, Continuum Press, New York, New York, 1994.

74 Thomas Merton, *The Silent Life*, Farrar, Straus and Giroux, New York, New York, 1957, p. 167.

75 RSV Bible, Romans 8:26.

76 *The Sacred Pipe*, p. 34 ff.

77 Soren Kierkegaard, *Purity of Heart Is to Will One Thing*, Harper Torchbacks, New York, New York, 1956, p. 51.

78 Marcus Borg in *God at 2000*, Morehouse Pub., Harrisburg, Pennsylvania, 2000, pp. 25-26.

79 Transcribed from audio tape *I Want Burning: The Ecstatic World of Rumi, Hafiiz, and Lalla*, Coleman Barks, Sounds True Recordings, Boulder, Colorado, 1992.

80 Thomas Merton, *The Wisdom of the Desert*, New Directions, New York, New York, 1960, p. 43.

81 Thomas Merton, *New Seeds*, p. 223.

82 Henri Nouwen, *The Way of the Heart*, The Seabury Press, New York, New York, 1981, p. 28.

83 Thomas Merton, *New Seeds*, p. 15.

84 *The Sacred Pipe*, p. 43.

85 RSV Christian Bible, Amos: 5:21.

86 All Psalms from Revised Standard Version of Christian Bible.

87 Thomas Merton, *New Seeds*, p. 18.

88 Thomas Merton, *New Seeds*, p. 19.

89 Barks, pp. 141-142.

90 Barks, pp. 141-142.

91 Thomas Merton, *New Seeds*, p. 32.

92 Henri Nouwen, *Reaching Out*, Doubleday & Co. Garden City, New York, 1966, p. 19.

93 Nouwen, *Reaching Out*, p. 14.

94 Nouwen, *Reaching Out*, p. 17.

95 Howard and Edna Hong, trans./ed. *Sören Kierkegaard's Journals and Papers*, Vol. II, p. 397 ff. Princeton University Press (7 volumes) 1967-1978 in *Provocations*, Plough Pub. Press, 1999.

96 Nouwen, *Reaching Out*, p. 23.

97 Internet Source, author Jerry Ropelato HYPERLINK http://internet-filter-review. toptenreviews <http://internet-filter-review.toptenreviews.com/internet-pornography-statistics.html>

98 "Walden and Other Writings," (from *Life Without Principles*), Modern Library, New York, New York, 1937, pp. 73-74.

99 Many Buddhist stories are so ancient a specific source is difficult to cite. For a good introduction to Zen Buddhism *see* Dennis Genpo Merzel, *The Eye Never Sleeps: Striking to the Heart of Zen*, Shambala Publications, Inc., Boston, 1991.

100 Rainer Maria Rilkie, *Letters to a Young Poet*, Norton Pub., New York, New York, 1954, p. 59.

101 Soygal Rinpoche, *Tibetan Book of Living and Dying*, Harper Collins, New York, New York, 1994, p. 52.

102 Thomas Merton, *Thoughts in Solitude*, Noonday Press, New York, New York, 1958, p. 13.

103 Paul Gruchow, *The Necessity of Empty Spaces*, Milkweed Editions, Minneapolis, Minnesota, 1999, p. 147.

104 Rinpoche, p. 53.

105 Data from website of The School of Professional Psychology at Forest Institute Springfield Campus, 2885 W. Battlefield, Springfield, Missouri, 65807.

106 Ladinsky, *Love Poems*, p. 350.

107 *See* footnote 99.

108 Sylvia Boorstein, *It's Easier Than You Think: the Buddhist Way to Happiness*, Harper, San Francisco, California, 1997.

109 Quoting St. Ignatius of Loyola, from Richard Rohr Tape, *The Enneagram: The Discernment of Spirits*, February 25, 2008.

110 Anne Frank, *Anne Frank: The Diary of a Young Girl*, Bantem Books, New York, New York, 1993, p. 158.

## Selected Bibliography

The following books may serve as good companions on your spiritual journey.

| | |
|---|---|
| *Black Elk Speaks* | John Neihardt (ed.) |
| *Life's Journey—Zuya* | Albert White Hat, Sr. |
| *Mediations with Native American Lakota Spirituality* | Paul Steinmetz (ed.) |
| *The Essential Rumi* | Coleman Barks |
| *Rumi: Soul Fury* | Coleman Barks |
| *The Gift: Poetry of Hafiz* | Daniel Ladinsky |
| *Love Poems from God* | Daniel Ladinsky |
| *The Jew in the Lotus* | Roger Kaminsky |
| *A Book of Psalms: Selected and Adapted from the Hebrew* | Stephen Mitchell |
| *New Seeds of Contemplation* | Thomas Merton |
| *Thoughts in Solitude* | Thomas Merton |
| *The Wisdom of the Desert* | Thomas Merton |
| *Thirst* | Mary Oliver |
| *New and Selected Poems* | Mary Oliver |
| *The Womanspirit Sourcebook* | Patricia Wynne (ed.) |

## About the Author

Chet Meyers was born in Pittsburgh, Pennsylvania, where, as a child, he attended Smithfield Congregational Church and not infrequently interrupted Sunday School with his antics. He completed a B.A. in sociology at Allegheny College, a Methodist school, where he briefly flirted with atheism and naturalism. His graduate work was at Yale University, where he earned a Master of Divinity and re-established his religious roots in Christianity. On graduating from seminary, Chet and his wife moved to Minneapolis, Minnesota, where they were part of an alternative church model, and later sojourned with the Quakers for several years. After four years' work with urban youth and serving as a peace intern with the American Friends Service Committee, Chet joined the faculty of Metropolitan State University where, for thirty-two years, he taught courses in education, philosophy, spirituality, and natural science to adult students. Currently, he is a member of the Spirit of St. Stephen's Catholic Community, an intentional congregation focused on social justice issues. Chet has spoken and led workshops on teaching adult students at over two dozen U.S. colleges and universities. He is an avid fisherman, birder, and wildflower gardener. His publications of over forty articles and six books include *Teaching Students to Think Critically* (Jossey Bass, 1986), *Promoting Active Learning in the College Classroom* (with Thomas Jones, Jossey Bass, 1993), *Bass: A Handbook of Strategies* (with Al Lindner et. al., Al Lindner Outdoors, Inc., 1981), and *First College: A Reflective Journal* (Metropolitan State University, 1999).